ACADEMIC EXCELLENCE THROUGH EQUITY

WHEN MONEY TALKS

Sis Opal,
Thanks for your support

[signature]

GLENFORD DUFFUS

Tellwell Talent
www.tellwell.ca

ISBN
978-0-2288-5785-3 (Hardcover)
978-0-2288-5786-0 (Paperback)
978-0-2288-5784-6 (eBook)

CONTENTS

LIST OF DIAGRAMS AND FIGURES

PREFACE

Globally, poverty is experienced by diverse groups in society. Our schools and classrooms mirror social milieu. As a result, in classrooms around the world, student populations portraying economic disadvantage are observable and documented phenomena. Consequently, school leadership must be transformative, school improvement plans should be developed with social justice and equity at the centre; there should be recognition of diversity that exists in both students and staff and that both students and staff should view their diversity as strength and capitalize on the available proficiency to enhance learning and growth. A key ingredient in this partnership is growth mindset (Dweck, 2006). The growth mindset should permeate all school and classroom interactions and practices.

In the school environment, leaders must believe they need to collaborate with teachers to share and develop expertise. Teachers believe they know their students' learning needs and have the expertise to support their achievement. Teachers also intentionally pursue opportunities to get better at what they do recognizing the constant changing populations of students they teach. Teachers' knowledge of their students should encompass data about the environment and lived experiences students bring to the classroom.

I have taught, led and supervised many schools in many jurisdictions that serve students from poor communities. I have observed and noted the challenges, frustrations, apathy, self-fulfilling prophecies, attempts at becoming more effective, sense of accomplishment and constant striving for equity and excellence. My observations have triggered many years of research on what successful schools do differently. My practice as teacher, principal and superintendent of education turning around under-achieving schools has been significantly shaped by my own research and from research studies by outstanding scholars in the field as well. This book is a representation of some of the best practices employed by educators serving students living in poverty.

With the persistent increase in the number of students living in poverty coupled with community pressure to improve academic achievement for all learners, educational leaders have been pursuing initiatives to enhance success for all their students. This book presents literature on the correlation between academic achievement and socio-economic status. The book also examines transformative leadership, instructional practices and professional learning communities (PLCs) as strategies to enhance academic achievement for students from poor communities. The book is intended to support educators in their attempts to accomplish enhanced academic achievement for all learners. As well, policy makers can capitalize on the content to support policies and practices on leadership and teacher professional development. Faculties of Education can use the findings to inform and shape their teacher education programs.

Keywords: Instructional practices, transformative leadership, academic achievement, learning opportunity index, professional development, professional learning communities, equity, poverty.

ACKNOWLEDGEMENTS

I wish to express my sincere appreciation to my wife, Janette, my children, Demane, Kimarie Joseph, Ian and Melissa for believing, motivating and supporting me, thank you. You have been my tower of strength. The completion of this book is your success.

CHAPTER ONE

INTRODUCTION

As an educator leading schools serving students living in poverty in different jurisdictions, I have always wondered why some of these schools experience excellent student academic achievement while others serving a similar population of students seemed to be mired in underachievement. This curiosity has helped to shape my exploration, belief and efforts to deliver equitable learning outcomes for all learners. This belief is predicated on the fact that students come to the learning environment with diverse achievement levels, from diverse backgrounds and experiences and possess diverse motivation to learning. This awareness has presented significant challenges- how to create access to equitable learning opportunities for all students especially those from economically disadvantaged communities, how to also offer opportunities and explore program initiatives, instructional strategies and professional learning opportunities in an attempt to maximize achievement outcomes for all in these diverse environments.

My focus and energy could have been expended on what seemed to be formidable challenges that could suppress my passion and drive for excellence. However, the challenge of changing the trajectory from under-achievement for students of a socio-economically disadvantaged community to an achievement of excellent learning outcomes presented a growth opportunity for me. As a principal promoted to my first

Canadian school, I collected and disaggregated data on students' demographics (gender, special needs learners, English proficiency), school community characteristics (median family income, family receiving social assistance, lone parent families, and parental level of education), school processes (programs, student placements, staffing and timetabling) student learning (formative and summative assessment tools and evaluation outcomes) instructional practices aimed at improving achievement and perception (beliefs, values and attitudes that characterized the learning environment) and achievement. The evidence gleaned from the data analysis was insightful and provoked a sense of urgency to work with staff to effect changes in student academic achievement. Knowing and understanding these student data, helped in my attempt to develop a transformative learning environment by incorporating students' experiences and learning needs. The review of the data prompted me to establish a multidisciplinary team of staff as an approach to engage staff, add divergent thinking to the analyses and discussions, consequently, better informing the decisions and strategic direction. The team therefore was comprised of administrators and staff from all departments and echelons in the school.

The data analyses undertaken by the multidisciplinary team allowed staff to delineate perceived variables that impact on student achievement (attendance, behavior, motivation, interest) and to make decisions on the variables on which the school has the most direct control- teaching and learning. The analyses also provided crucial information on external factors that had potential to adversely impact on achievement, gaps in learning outcomes, assessment and instructional practices, teaching expertise, possible strategies to build teaching capacity as well as the collaborative approaches needed to effect enhanced student achievement.

This first step in developing a "school achievement planning process" expanded my learning curve and I believe that of the vice principals and the entire staff. We were offered significant learning opportunity, that of careful and frank reflections on instructional practices- identifying practices perceived to be effective, ones to be improved and ones to be abandoned. Leadership practices were also scrutinized and informed decisions made to effect needed changes. Also, administrators and teachers identified resident expertise, needed additional assistance and explored strategies to incorporate and develop collaborative expertise.

As the team leader, I encouraged a review of the organizational structure, logistics, collective agreements, policies and procedures and used the information to shape the school's improvement model. Greater staff involvement was facilitated and encouraged through the establishment of various sub-committees: data management, staff development, student attendance, discipline and monitoring, and student motivation.

As a school we focused on using staff development as a vehicle to improve instructional practices and to achieve equitable learning outcomes for the entire diverse student population. As the school leader, I engaged staff in researching, developing and implementing a focused, intentional and effective professional learning community (PLC). Within a three year period, students' academic achievement improved significantly. I wondered whether the focus on transformative leadership and the use of professional learning communities (PLCs) to develop and change instructional practices contributed to the enhanced academic achievement the school experienced. Consequently, this study has sought to examine transformative leadership and professional learning communities (PLCs) as possible variables to enhance academic achievement in schools serving students from poor communities. This book seeks to shed lights on the following practices:

1. Transformative leadership practices employed by high performing schools to improve academic achievement for students living in poverty.
2. Strategies employed by principals and teachers in order to develop leadership and build instructional capacity to enhance academic achievement for economically disadvantaged students.
3. Instructional practices that characterize high performing schools serving students from poor communities.

The book purports that transformative leadership can positively impact academic achievement for students living in poverty. Hess and

Kelly (2007) say, "School leadership is the key to school improvement" (p.244). Their work focuses on the transformational leadership style which characterizes the principal's leadership attributes as managing school improvement using data, motivating and influencing teachers, collaborating on curriculum innovation and pedagogy as well as providing coaching support. These attributes should auger well for the principal in leading the school improvement process. However, as the challenge to provide equitable access to learning opportunities and to achieve equitable leaning outcomes for marginalized learners become more evident and pronounced, there is an urgency to focus on the transformative leadership style.

The transformative leadership seeks to address social justice issues such as stereotypes, prejudices, discrimination and barriers to achievement. It embraces the idea that leadership resides in teacher educators and not just the principal. In an environment where students from economically disadvantaged background are underachieving and there is an outcry from many advocates for improvement, school leaders must take bold transformative actions. This book emphasizes transformative leadership that addresses social justice perspectives, recognizes the diversity of our students and the changes necessary to achieve equity for all learners. Transformative leadership is crucial to changing underachievement to high achievement for students living in poverty.

Studies done in other jurisdictions link poverty to constructs related to learning outcomes such as dropout rate, student behaviour, retention, high school readiness, cognitive development, graduation rate and receptive vocabulary tests (Levin, 2007; Kagan, 1992; Thomas, 2007; Willims, 2007; Brooks-Gunn and Duncan, 2007 and McLeod 1998.) However, from my research it was concluded that transformative leadership (principal) practices can still make a difference in achievement outcomes. The research study also shows that professional learning communities (PLCs) are strategies to develop leadership and collaboration as well as build instructional capacity.

Description and Significance of Problem

Poverty is a challenging construct to define with any sense of clarity because of the frequent shifts in the many variables that have ramifications for its definition. This study uses the Statistics Canada definition which considers families to be living in poverty when their income falls below 50% of the median household income. The Low-Income Measures for single parents with one child was $28,185.00 after taxes (October, 2014).

According to the *Toronto District School Board Urban Diversity Strategy: on Student Achievement* (2008), "Many societal factors contribute to the marginalization of communities, families and students--factors such as poverty, racism, sexism, classism and so on" (p.2). Poverty impacts on students' learning and on the curricular opportunities schools provide to improve academic achievement. Poverty sometimes has impact on readiness for learning, gaps in learning, student class placement and the rigor of the curriculum to which they are exposed. If students are streamed into low level program opportunities and experience ineffective instruction, the likely outcome will be underachievement. However, the fact that there are many factors that influence learning cannot be overstated.

Jensen (2009) cites research studies that link poverty to: absenteeism (Johnson-Brooke, Lewis, Evans, Whalen, Drevets and Schulkin 2003), reduced cognition, creativity, motivation, determination and effort (Johnson 1981), and learning (Blankstein and Noguera, 2015). Other studies link poverty to increased risk of dropping out of school and to health, behavioural and emotional problems. (Mistry, Vandewater, Huston and McIloyd 2002). These studies link poverty to variables that impact on learning outcomes and academic achievement. Yet, an analysis of EQAO results reveals that some schools serving significant student population living in poverty perform at or above provincial standards. Although many schools are serving a significant number of students from poor communities, some of these schools seem to perform above expectations. This motivated my desire to explore the reasons these schools do well despite the economic challenges their students face. It is my belief that student achievement is not determined by their SES, but by the quality of learning accomplished through a synergy of leadership, and professional learning communities (PLCs) that facilitates the development of effective instructional practice.

Schools may not have the propensity to directly increase or decrease the level of poverty experienced by individuals residing in the communities where they are located. However, through value-added educational opportunities, experiences resulting in high levels of academic achievement, schools can positively influence life chances for students from economically disadvantaged communities. Hoy, Tarter and Hoy (2006) state that a school with "high academic optimism" (p.22) is a collectivity in which the faculty believes it can make a difference, that students can learn and high academic performance can be achieved. This implies that if all staff work collaboratively with a focus on high student achievement, this effort will produce exceptional results. Consequently, schools should expend their efforts and resources on indirectly changing the outcomes of poverty by achieving academic excellence for all learners.

A closer examination of the impact of poverty on academic achievement therefore, is pertinent in any search for policies, approaches or strategies that can influence systemic outcomes. Poverty is one of the many variables that impact on academic achievement. There is a preponderance of evidence in research done in other Canadian jurisdictions (Coughlan, 2017; Burton, Phipps and Zhang, 2013; Volante, Schnepf, Jerrim and Klinger, 2018), the United States (Ainsworth, 2002; Evans, 2004; Fagan,2017) and Europe (Carey, 2018 and Azzolini and Contini, 2016) that links poverty to academic achievement, cognitive gaps, school readiness, retention and behaviour among other variables. Although some of the research studies use the variables "socioeconomic status" instead of poverty, the conclusions drawn from the analysis of the data portray remarkable similarities that render logical inferring valid.

Ferguson et. al. (2007) state, "Canadian research confirms poverty's negative influence on student behaviour, achievement and retention in school" (p. 701). These writers also suggest that persistent socioeconomic disadvantage has negative impact on the life outcomes of many Canadian children. "The reality, in the Program for International Student Assessment (PISA) and in every other assessment of student outcome", Levin (2007) argues, "is that socioeconomic status remains the most powerful single influence on students' educational and other life outcomes. This is true in Finland, and Canada as well as in the United States and everywhere else" (p.75).

Although the findings from the research studies indicate the negative correlation between poverty and academic achievement and identify socioeconomic status as a powerful influence, the findings have not established causation. While the influence is powerful, there is optimism that change is possible. My knowledge of powerful influential factors has informed my decision making on implementing strategies that seemed to have made a difference.

Studies that originate from the "vulnerability index" (1991) created from the National Longitudinal Study of Children and Youth (NLSCY) have repeatedly shown that socioeconomic factors have significant pervasive and persistent influence on academic achievement. Phipps and Lethbridge (2006) found that socioeconomic disadvantage and other risk factors that are associated with poverty (e.g. lower parental education and high family stress) have negative effects on cognitive development and academic achievement. Conversely, these studies claim that higher incomes were consistently associated with better outcomes for children. Some authors, Isaacs and Magnuson (2011) further explore the cognitive domain using Peabody Picture Vocabulary Score (PPVT) and standard math and reading tests scores. From their findings, they conclude that low-income children have lower than average scores (-0.246 of a standard deviation) while affluent children have higher scores (+0.256 of a standard deviation) in reading.

The evidence is substantive that affluent students outperform students in poverty in many subject areas. The National Assessment of Educational Process (NAEP, 2005) reported that 13% of children living in poverty scored proficiency, compared to 40% of students who were from affluent backgrounds. Students living in poverty also scored 40% below the threshold of basic competency while 21% of students not living in poverty have scores in a similar threshold. NEAP test results for grades 4, 8 and 12 students from economic disadvantage backgrounds were lowest in math, reading, writing and science. Other studies by Ma and Klinger (2000), Willms (2002), and Entraf and Minoui (2005) have also established links between academic, cognitive and behavioural outcomes and poverty. The links established by these and other studies are clear indications that educators cannot lose sight of the reality that many variables impact on achievement. Variables such as home environment (limited or lack of resources, affordability of out of school programs and opportunities) contribute to gaining previous knowledge and closing achievement gaps. These opportunities can be safely linked to family income. However, in spite of the challenges faced by some of our students and their families, our schools are still viewed as the only hope of making a difference in their situation by making the difference in learning outcomes.

International studies have also consistently shown similar associations between socioeconomic measures and academic outcomes. For example, the Progress in International Reading Literacy Study (PIRLS, 2011) assessed the comprehensive literacy skills for grade 4 students in 35 countries. The Program for International Student Assessment (PISA) assessed reading, math and science scores of 15-year old students in 43 countries (OECD Technical Report, 2000). The reports indicate a significant relationship between SES and educational measures in all countries. The report states that there is support for the conclusion that income or SES has significant effects on educational attainment in elementary school through high school inferred from the PIRLS and PISA data.

Evidence from other research has established the connection between poverty and school readiness. A child's ability to succeed academically and socially in school requires appropriate motor development, age-appropriate social knowledge, competence, language skills and cognitive skills. However, one of the factors that impacts on child development and school readiness is poverty. (Ferguson, Bovaird and Mueller, 2007; Isaacs, (2012). The evidence therefore points to the home environment as a significant contributor to school readiness. The resources, support

8

and training afforded pre-school children can greatly enhance their level of readiness. Conversely, the lack or limitation of resources, support and training can also impede readiness and consequently, school success or academic achievement.

Many Canadian studies have documented links between low-income households and decreased school readiness. Thomas (2007) reported that children from lower income households score significantly lower on measures of vocabulary and communication skills, knowledge of numbers, copying and symbol use, ability to concentrate and cooperative play with other children from higher income households. Also, Willms (2007) concluded that children from lower socioeconomic status (SES) households score lower on a receptive vocabulary test than higher SES children. As a result of these findings, there is evidence that some children begin formal schooling with gaps in their academic achievement. However, in spite of the "achievement gap", schools through the use of effective instructional practices can interrupt the achievement disadvantage and create learning opportunities for these students to succeed and meet high expectations. The leadership of the school is crucial in creating these learning opportunities.

According to Bass and Faircloth (2013) leaders performing these roles champion high academic expectations for students and ensure teachers receive high-quality professional development, mentoring and guidance necessary to provide students with opportunities and resources to learn and achieve similarly to or exceeding their peers. The format, content and strategies were assessed and fine tuned to meet emergent needs. The principal and the teachers become learners, took responsibilities for their learning, and developed accountability for the group's learning and enhanced student achievement. Professional learning communities (PLCs) can be instrumental in changing the mindsets of teachers and students regarding their influence on teaching and learning and how this influence can result in successful teaching and enhanced learning.

The challenge to change mindsets of staff who had succumbed to the negative beliefs about students and their limitation to achieve high levels of academic achievement, consoled themselves that they had done all they could, and students who believed that their circumstances determined their destiny, can become real, sometimes daunting and seemingly insurmountable. However, capitalizing on my experiences in different areas and jurisdictions, drawing on the expertise of colleagues making a difference for students from poor communities, my observation, passion for equitable access and opportunities for all learners, I proceeded to be engaged in the change process with great optimism. The revelatory knowledge developed in undertaking my responsibilities as principal and then as superintendent of education has shaped my belief that equity and inclusivity are mutual frameworks to pursue enhanced student academic achievement.

This belief has catapulted my optimism to new height and significantly reshaped my practice to include greater teacher leadership and collaboration as a key ingredient to producing successful learning outcomes. I have learned to embrace the practice of developing what is referred to as "the human side of the enterprise" (McGregor, 1960), creating opportunities for staff to feel valued, knowing that they make significant contributions to student achievement and the development of their colleagues. I have provided opportunities to celebrate successes, reflect on failures and strategize on different and new initiatives as important components of leadership. The components of the practice that resulted in phenomenal improvement to student achievement included a renewed focus on leadership, and professional learning communities (PLCs).

The process undertaken and the results accomplished have led me to believe that principals working collaboratively with teachers in creating learning opportunities for staff and students can develop teacher expertise and improve academic performance of students. The results were not only encouraging, but have strengthened my belief that focused instructional practices centred on the needs of all learners, supported by innovative, supportive and collaborative leadership that creates and implements staff development opportunities can positively impact on the achievement of economically disadvantaged students.

Schools' primary focus is student achievement. Recognizing that schools serve diverse learners, some of whom come to the learning environment from families living in poverty, schools have been assiduously pursuing strategies to change the trajectory from one that leads from poverty to low achievement to one of enhanced academic achievement. While poverty adversely impacts on academic achievement, poverty does not have to be the determining factor on learning outcomes or academic achievement. Education has the potential to be the great equalizer and offers the greatest prospect to positively impact academic outcomes. As a result, educators constantly confront the challenge of maximizing learning outcomes for all learners, but especially students living in poverty.

Despite the challenges faced by teachers working with students from low SES background, schools have been exploring instructional strategies to improve their learning outcomes by focusing on the quality of learning opportunities rather than on learning deficits. It must be acknowledged that students living in poverty, or who come from poor communities, are not a demographically homogenous group and therefore have diverse learning needs. Meeting these diverse and complex learning needs presents additional challenges to the schools in general and the classroom teachers more specifically. Research studies indicate that the classroom teacher has a greater impact on student achievement than parents or poverty (Hanushek, 2005; Haycock, 1998; Rockoff, 2004). Hattie (2012) in highlighting the literature review and meta-analysis done in collaboration with Richard Jaeger (1998) identified five major dimensions of excellent or expert teachers:

> Expert teachers have high levels of knowledge and understanding of the subjects they teach, can guide learning to describable surface and deep outcomes, can successfully monitor learning and provide feedback that assists students for progress, can attend to the more attitudinal attributes of learning (especially developing self-efficacy and mastery of motivation), and can provide defensible evidence of positive impacts of the teaching on student learning (p.24).

This description implies that the synergy between curriculum, pedagogy or instructional practice, assessment and evaluation strategies and the inter connectedness of the various aspects of the teachers' work, contributes to academic achievement. Through assessment and evaluation strategies, teachers learn more about student learning needs.

My analysis finds that this research needs to be analyzed in the context of students' backgrounds, experiences, family economic status and community challenges. Comprehensive knowledge of students, their families and community should inform curriculum development and instructional practices. Giroux (1988a) opines that teachers should possess the knowledge, skills, values and attitudes to understand, interrogate inequities and act as change agents. According to Howard (2006) this knowledge includes knowing my practice: curriculum, pedagogy, instructional design, developmental psychology, history and philosophy of education. It includes knowing my students: cultures, racial identities, language, family backgrounds, home situations, learning characteristics, economic status, strengths, challenges and uniqueness. Thirdly this knowledge must include knowledge of "self". How does one's world view impact on the delivery of academic opportunities and the leading of achievement outcomes? The knowledge of practice, students and self and how these aspects intersect in the learning environment to maximize achievement is transformative and necessary. Howard (ibid.) says, "Transformationist pedagogy means teaching and leading in such a way that more of our students, across more of their differences, achieve at a higher level more of the time without giving up who they are" (p. 133). Education in Canada reflects affluent perspectives and values. Curriculum chiefly personifies content and pedagogy that students from poorer backgrounds seldom can identify. Marginalized students find very little that reflects or celebrates their cultures, heroes of their heritage, draws on their strengths and evokes their interests (Kilgour, 1994). The implication is that curriculum and pedagogy are connected to culture and economics of the larger societal values and may unintentionally portray biases. These biases instead of producing high academic achievement for all learners may well be hindrance to that achievement.

In spite of the Ministry of Education's prescribed curriculum and its grade level learning outcomes, there is room to adapt localized content and implement teacher determined teaching strategies. This scenario creates opportunities for principals and teachers to collaborate on strategies that best meet the needs of all their students and to incorporate curricular content and activities reflecting students and their culture positively, creating opportunities to validate students' strengths -- deepening their knowledge, understanding and expanding their thinking. In a study of high performing high poverty schools, Kannapel et.al. (2005) find that successful leaders ensure alignment between curriculum and instruction and provide time for teachers to analyze student data in an attempt to respond to individualized learning needs.

These well-researched, documented and practised elements should be present in all learning environments. The intent, however, is not to portray the teacher as a "super-person" with knowledge and effective strategies to individually transform all learners. The extent to which instructional practices and learning intersect in each classroom may vary significantly. Ineffective instructional practices result in underachievement while effective practices may result in enhanced academic achievement. However, educators are always reflecting on their practices and pursuing opportunities for growth. Educators are always seeking to acquire mastery of their subject knowledge and develop pedagogical expertise. Educators also recognize that no one individual has all the answers to address effectively the divergent needs learners from poor communities bring to the learning environment. Consequently, there is a shift from individuals working independently to individuals working collaboratively in developing their competence. Consistent, high-quality instruction in every classroom happens when teachers are engaged in peer observations and the sharing of effective teaching strategies (Goodwin, 2011).

Professional learning communities are possible vehicles to facilitate teachers broadening their knowledge base and their effectiveness. Bass and Faircloth (2013) state that by implementing appropriate professional learning opportunities, teachers are better equipped to meet the needs of all students, perform more effectively and are more likely to remain in the profession for a longer time. This stability should augur well for economically disadvantaged students who sometimes experience many transitions. Teachers, as educational practitioners, in professional learning communities can develop leadership expertise and serve as mentors to inexperienced teachers and teachers new to the school. Zapeda (2008) purports that teachers must be empowered to exercise their voices and school leaders should be responsive to those voices and align professional development activities with the organizational learning needs of the school and its staff. Leaders can create the environment for teachers to learn from their peers through formalized professional development and mentorship. The aim of these opportunities should be instructional capacity building. The school's diverse learners should be the beneficiaries.

Recognizing that there is diversity of learning needs in any student group and "that one size does not fit all" requires that each teacher in each classroom be engaged intentionally and consistently in a practice of treating students differently based on their individual learning needs. Fullan (2009) characterizes this form of differentiation as personalized learning. The practice, he explains, requires that instruction and learning supports be modified to meet the varied learning needs and disposition of highly diverse student bodies. Leadbeater (2002) refers to this practice as "putting the learner at the heart of the education system" (p.1). In a classroom where students are placed at the centre of learning, curriculum and resources positively portray the learners and their ancestral contributions to society; teachers employ pedagogy that addresses differentiated learning needs and are cognizant of each learner's previous knowledge and readiness. This pedagogy should capitalize greatly on authentic diagnostic and formative assessment data in order to inform the practice.

In addition, this information should be used to determine students' progress and intervention strategies that facilitate enhanced academic achievement. If students' learning must be maximized, especially for those learners from poor communities, high quality pedagogy must be the hallmark of all classrooms and cannot be restricted to the fortunate or privileged few. Consequently, the effectiveness of a school's instructional practices is characterized by the successful learning outcomes of all its students, not just some of its students. Therefore, high quality learning must be experienced in all classrooms. Fullan, Hill and Crevola, (2006) posited a model of teacher capacity building called "The Triple P"- "personalization, precision of response to the learners need and professional learning on the part of all teachers" (p. 15) aimed at making this experience a reality for all learners.

While personalization refers to individualization of the instruction, precision recognizes the importance of developing competence and mastery of a few practices. The mastery of these practices involves clear and specific knowledge of students' previous achievement, tailored intervention that engages students in the particular learning and continuous assessment and instruction in dialogue with the students as appropriate. It is clear from the review of the literature that the effectiveness of this model hinges on the synergy of the component parts and the development of teacher collective capacity. However, the level of under-achievement experienced by many of our schools implies that either students' previous achievement or continuous assessment dialogues are not part of their learning experiences or the application of strategies is ineffectively applied.

Students' Needs and Schools' Delivery

Hattie (2009, p.111) synthesises over 800 meta-analyses of teaching practices related to student engagement and achievement. He concludes that structured feedback to students, reciprocal teaching (teaching students to learn cognitive strategies to facilitate their own learning), observation and feedback on one's own teaching are strategies that have high impact on student learning. If effective, sustainable, instructional practices facilitate learning for all and are crucial in enhancing academic achievement, the challenge then, is how to build capacity, facilitate instructional change or influence instructional practices and develop leadership that makes this learning outcome possible.

To begin to address this very important question requires schools generally and teachers and principals more specifically to change leadership and professional development direction, and shift instructional focus. The leadership of the school's administrators is crucial to the effective functioning of the school. These leaders have responsibility for leading the school operations and ensuring staff development and student achievement. However, there needs to be the recognition that teachers possess leadership expertise and a conscious and deliberate attempt made to utilize this expertise in an environment of shared leadership. This approach to leadership could represent a change in paradigm for many individuals. Also, a careful evaluation of instructional practices should be done by principals and teachers and the necessary changes made in order to meet apparent student learning needs. Some strategies may need to be changed while others may need to be intensified. There must also be the recognition of both those external variables, like poverty, which schools cannot directly control and internal variables, such as instructional practices within the classroom, over which there is direct influence.

Curtis and City (2009) find:

> In school systems that are improving and succeeding in helping children learn, people embrace the notion that what they do matters, focus on improving what they can control rather ....what they can't control, and look at student learning data ...... as information, not as a commentary on their personal value (p.13).

At the heart of this stance, is a belief in taking responsibility for personal actions.

Principals take responsibility to provide leadership in staff development and teachers take responsibility for helping students learn. To change the trajectory from a belief that students can learn to provide the opportunities to making this a reality, requires an atmosphere that is non-judgmental and collaborative. Continuous reflection and learning therefore, are at the core of improved learning outcomes for all learners.

In a professional development environment, student assessment, demographic and community characteristics data can be drawn on to inform instructions and centre students in the heart of the learning process. The understanding developed from the correct interpretation of the data should inform what the school does.

These student data that drive actions should identify students from poor neighbourhoods and any perceived challenges associated with this reality such as limited opportunities, level of readiness and motivation for learning. The knowledge gleaned from the study of student data should not engender stereotypes, negative perceptions or deficit thinking that could adversely impact on learning opportunities and outcomes. Rather, this knowledge should assist in the creation of differentiated opportunities reflecting high expectations for all learners. Bomer, May and Semingson (2009) believe that deficit thinking damages relationships between teachers and students and promotes lower level achievement and lower quality instruction. The intent is not to focus on individual teacher competence or lack thereof, but on the collective willingness to strive for learning for all.

Dweck (2006) defines and describes two mindsets "growth" and "fixed". Learners with a growth mindset are those who believe that they can learn just about anything, can accept struggles and failure and understand that with effort and perseverance, they can succeed. Conversely, those with a fixed or deficit mindset might believe that they have a predetermined level of intelligence, skill or talents. Both of these mindsets have significant ramifications not only for the learners, but for the teachers. Regardless of students' experience and level of accomplishment on entering the learning environment, teachers must believe that they can learn, use a variety of data sources to identify their learning needs, employ instructional practices that differentiate content, product, process, assessment, and opportunities for remediation in response to each learner's most apparent learning needs. Classrooms in which these instructional practices are evident and implemented are bound to accrue successful dividend for students living in poverty (Bass et. al., 2013, Jensen, 2017).

Levin (2008) believes that high expectations for all students, greater student engagement and motivation, a rich and engaging formal and informal curriculum and effective teaching practices in all classrooms on a daily basis are essential practices for improved outcomes. While these essential practices do not provide answers to all the questions teachers have regarding achieving successful learning outcomes, these considerations can augment other beliefs and strategies. However, all actions to enhance academic achievement should aim to achieve equitable opportunities for each learner to maximize his or her potentials. Since teachers for the most part are reflective practitioners, this positive characteristic combined with knowledge acquired from continuous learning should help enhance the effectiveness of the instructions. If schools therefore, are to be successful in achieving high academic achievement for students from low socioeconomic background, then student centred learning must be their number one priority. Schools cannot be fully satisfied with their accomplishments if only some students achieve success. They must undertake the responsibility for learning for all and measure the extent to which they are fulfilling their responsibility by the yardstick of successful learning outcomes for all their learners. The instructional strategies, assessment tools and the level of learning for each learner may vary significantly at the end of a lesson or unit. However, the question is what additional opportunities can be provided to support the learners who have not yet achieved the achievement goals? Here, the emphasis must be placed on the congruence of assessment and instruction to meet and maximize learning for each student.

In professional learning communities (PLCs) educators can collaborate on the analysis of student data, share evidence of their instructional practices on student achievement and be intentional in their focus and direction as a team. It is established that transformative leadership and professional learning communities can be instrumental in achieving successful learning outcomes for students from poor communities.

A review of the literature on "leadership" and "Professional Learning Communities (PLCs)" has provided insights on these very important variables. PLCs provide opportunities for principals and teachers to explore together, principles of system thinking and transformative leadership style and behaviours in order to examine and inform learning focus (Stinson, 2017, p.5). Transformative leaders model the style and strategies they want their staff to employ. They model risk taking, collaboration, a focus on learning and a focus on results (Erkens and Twadell, 2012, p.23). Student learning is positively affected by the quality of the professional learning of adults and the quality of professional learning in the school which should not be left to chance (Eaker and Keating, 2009, p. 50).

Poverty's Impact on Academic Achievement

Despite universal access to education in Canada, student achievement in schools is not a given. Reports point to the alarming increase in the number of children living in poverty in Canada generally, and in Toronto in particular. According to Monsebraaten (2013), "Alarmingly, thirty- eight point two (38.2) percent of children of single mothers in Ontario are living in poverty" (p. 1). She also mentions that Toronto holds onto its shameful title of "Child Poverty Capital of Canada" and that 28.6% of children in Toronto live in low-income households. The article further claims that eight of the city's neighbourhoods with the highest concentration of child poverty are in the city's north-west and five are in downtown. Schools in the areas specified are located in the Toronto District School Board (TDSB).

In the Toronto District School Board, schools are ranked according to the Learning Opportunity Index (LOI). The LOI is a measure of external challenges affecting student success that includes: median income, percentage of families whose income is below the income measure (before tax), percentage of families receiving social assistance, adults with low level of education, adults with university degrees and lone-parent families. The school with the greatest level of external challenges is ranked first on the index. On the other hand, the school with the least level of external challenges is ranked lowest. The schools in this study represent family income between $39,000.00 and

$40,000.00. Between fifty-three percent (53%) and fifty-seven percent (57%) earn family income below the Low Income Measure and between thirty-three percent (33%) and thirty-nine percent (39%) receive social assistance.

An analysis of the demographic and school community characteristics data collected from schools in the sample revealed that there are no significant differences between the schools on median family income, family income below the income measure, families receiving social assistance, lone parent families, adults with low level of education or even adults with high level of education. Schools also portray close similarities on the demographic attributes. Therefore, the minor differences on some of the demographic and school community characteristics, are not significant enough to skew the achievement reflected in the schools' EQAO results.

However, despite the increase in poverty and its ramification for educational attainment, our schools are still poised with the capabilities to transform adversity into successful learning outcomes. To support this claim, my study is organized by a central research question: Can leadership and professional learning communities make the difference in academic achievement for students living in poverty? This research project has afforded me the opportunity to test observations from my practice and possible connect them to theories in order to help facilitate school and system improvement.

In order to provide the information to be shared in this book, a research was conducted. This involved a questionnaire that was administered to 129 teachers in five schools. The principal of each school was invited to participate in a 60 minute audio-taped interview. Student demographic, school community characteristics and EQAO assessment data for students in the schools was collected, analyzed and used to determine similarities and or differences if any, between student population and achievement. The data was collected and analyzed using descriptive statistics and Pearson Product Moment Correlation Coefficient.

Summary

Chapter one has provided an overview of the book. This chapter has also served to highlight the impact of poverty on academic achievement, the challenges schools face in enhancing this achievement and the urgency and importance of exploring and documenting variables successful schools have used to demonstrate accountability for high academic results.

Chapter two provides the contextual framework: a review of the literature on Equity education and the need for professional learning communities (PLCs). This chapter also explores the meaning of equity in the context of academic achievement, systemic initiatives in Ontario to achieve equitable learning outcomes for all students, the gaps in achievement that persist for some learners and the need for professional learning communities (PLCs) to support instructional practice and policy directions aimed at achieving academic achievement for all students.

Chapter three presents a literature review on poverty, race and student achievement in relation to transformative leadership. Chapter four highlights Professional Learning Communities PLCs) as propositions to build and sustain leadership and instructional strategies.

Chapter five describes some professional development opportunities.

Chapter six highlights some proven pedagogical approaches utilized by schools to enhance academic achievement for students from poor communities.

CHAPTER TWO

CONCEPTUAL FRAMEWORK

Sociological, psychological, environmental and socio-economical factors shape the diversity of our student population. Students bring diverse characteristics to their learning which influence the way learning takes place and the final outcome as well. A combination of all or any of these factors can have either a powerful positive or adverse impact on achievement. Not only do these factors external to the classroom, impact on learning, but also certain internal classroom factors. This implies that relevant and rigorous curriculum delivered with differentiated instructional strategies must be informed by the demographic and community characteristics data that describe students' lived experiences. These experiences are crucial to understanding students' level of motivation, readiness to learn and intensity of the instruction (Bryk, Sebring, Allensworth, Luppescu and Easton, 2010). To achieve the maximum effectiveness of instruction and enhanced academic achievement may require educators to constantly and consistently seek to develop their expertise through additional professional development.

In each classroom, therefore, teachers are faced with the opportunity to create a synergy between individuality and collectivity in the delivery of curriculum, differentiated instructional and assessment practices in the vein of providing equitable access and opportunities for every student to achieve academic success. Individuality speaks to the idea that each student is unique and has individual strengths and learning needs. These needs are probably different from those of their other classmates and form part of the complexities in the learning environment. While this is true, individual students must learn and grow within a broader context. Consequently, the teacher may need to encourage cooperative or collective learning in order to enrich the experiences provided to all the learners. In addition, the students come from homes and communities with multiple experiences, cognitive abilities, language proficiencies, social and emotional well-being and different exposures or lack thereof to learning enrichment opportunities. These sociological and psychological factors help shape their uniqueness, but also are indicators of their strengths and needs. Identifying this diversity and incorporating the existing enormous strength in the learning environment, should yield dividend for both teachers and their students.

While these realities may present obstacles to academic achievement, they should not be viewed as defining learning outcomes. The learning opportunities our schools provide can make the difference between success and failure for these students.

These demographic and economic changes have ramifications for assessment and evaluation practices, pedagogy, curriculum, leadership, teacher preparedness and continuous development. School leaders and teachers must therefore use many (diagnostic, formative or summative) assessment tools and measures to identify students learning needs so that more informed decisions can be made about pedagogical practices. Since these factors influence learning outcomes for all learners, but more specifically students from economically disadvantaged backgrounds, it is imperative that a careful analysis of multiple data sources be undertaken to fully determine not only the complexities of work to be done, but the multiplicity and diversity of the teaching/learning strategies to be employed. Therefore, in addition to assessment data, a good understanding of student demographics and environmental information (parental income, level of education, access to educational opportunities, neighbourhood challenges such as violence, discrimination and even stereotypes and racism) should be pertinent in informing and shaping instructional practices. A comprehensive knowledge which includes information collected from formal and informal assessment should therefore influence instruction and curriculum as well as learning outcomes. This knowledge should allow teachers to view students not as empty vessels that come to the learning environment to be filled with knowledge dispensed by the teacher on the stage, but learners with strengths from previous knowledge that should be incorporated in the rich learning experiences to be created. It should be acknowledged that students from all backgrounds, socioeconomic statuses bring a wealth of knowledge to the learning tasks. In light of these findings my study engages Vygotsky's Zone of Proximal Development.

Vygotsky (1978) describes these factors as the role of social interaction in learning and development, the role of a more knowledgeable other in learning and the significance of the Zone of Proximal Development in learning.

Vygotsky (ibid.) deduced from his research that social interaction played an important role in learning and cognitive development and that learning is a social process originating with relationships with others before occurring with the individual. He subscribes to the idea of learning occurring in the Zone of Proximal Development (what the learner can do with or without help) and the role that a more knowledgeable other plays in the learning process. In the school context, the principal and the teachers are the "more knowledgeable other".

The concept of more knowledgeable other for the purpose of this book is linked to leadership acquiring knowledge about the diverse student population and using this knowledge to inform instructional practices and collaborate on the transformative leadership style in delivering professional learning communities (PLCs) aimed at intentionally improving academic achievement for economically disadvantaged learners. Since sociological, psychological and environmental factors shape our diverse student population and socialization impacts learning, the question is, what impact does having more knowledge have on achievement for students from poor communities and how can schools use this knowledge to enhance student learning? One should not view having knowledge on the learners as the panacea to producing equitable learning outcomes. However, armed with accurate information on students' learning needs should assist the teachers in the determination of appropriate intervention strategies.

In addition to the aforementioned categories of diversity, there are social, emotional, behavioural, mental, intellectual and physical diversity that characterize the richness in the classrooms. The challenge for teachers then, is how to be knowledgeable of this diversity, view it through the lens of richness, view it as an opportunity for growth and capitalize on the richness in providing equitable teaching and learning opportunities for all students to be successful. This challenge requires teachers and all individuals associated with producing high academic achievement to be on a path of continuously expanding their knowledge and constantly developing new skills in order to meet the diverse student learning needs. Andrews and Lupart (2015) say, "Diversity education is not just about the individual student, but also about the pedagogical, social, cultural, linguistic, and organizational elements within schools and classrooms. Diversity education is about both individuality and collectivity, where teachers and students within their classrooms view themselves as unique and as part of a group, where students engagement in learning is emphasized and connectedness between students, their peers and teachers is positive and promoted, and shared expectations for success are contagious and realized" (p.25). Capitalizing on that knowledge should enhance learning outcomes.

This implies that relevant and rigorous curriculum delivered with differentiated instructional strategies must be informed by demographic and school community characteristics data that describe students' lived experiences. These data are crucial to understanding students' level of motivation, readiness to learn and the intensity of the instruction to be used (Bryk et. al., 2010). To achieve the maximum effectiveness of instruction and enhanced academic achievement may require educators to constantly and consistently seek to develop their expertise through additional professional development.

According to Leinhardt (1992), there is an expectation that teachers know curriculum content and have a repertoire of pedagogical strategies. A combination of this expertise and a comprehensive knowledge of student learning needs should support the modification of curriculum to reflect positively the experiences of the students being taught. This positive reflection should create a sense of belonging, increase motivation and engagement and consequently, increase the level of achievement for all the learners. Curtis and City (2010) say:

> A strategy of improving instruction, developing a student assessment system, and creating a comprehensive student support system is a good example of a strategy that is focused, coherent, and synergetic. A comprehensive assessment system provides teachers with valuable information about student learning; this transformation then informs how teachers use the curriculum, the instructional materials, and their training to maximum effect (p.33).

The crux of the matter is how much do educational practitioners know their students and themselves (their level of expertise, strengths) and how this knowledge shapes their belief and expectations of students, the delivery of curriculum and quality of the teaching/learning opportunities they provided. Do teachers believe that all students can learn and that they have the expertise to make the difference? Educators must believe that not only some students can learn but all students can achieve successful learning outcomes. Students from economically disadvantage backgrounds have the potentials to learn and achieve as much and even more than their peers from more affluent backgrounds. The challenge, however, is how to be fully knowledgeable about the factors that impact on each of the many students in each classroom, their diverse learning needs, gaps in educational attainment, limited resources, neighbourhood and family challenges, different beliefs about learning and achievements among other variables and then collaborate on instructional practices and learning opportunities to achieve academic excellence. The solution to this challenge could be viewed as daunting or as growth opportunities for both students and educators. Therefore, knowing that these factors shape learning needs and should influence practices, should propel educators to seriously contemplate not equality, but equity.

Teachers undertake their responsibilities with different levels of expertise, beliefs about students and their learning needs and their abilities to make a difference. Their disposition will impact on their implementation of equitable practices. As a result, the schools in the sample have been implementing PLCs to effect changes to teacher practice and mindset. The principals in the sample schools when asked to identify strategies used by principal and teachers to address inequalities cited instructional practices, PLCs and leadership. Principal H says, "Staff realize the urgency…no time to take on deficit model… need to use rich tasks, differentiated instruction with multiple points in the activities. Lessons that have rich or high- level thinking tasks allow all students to be successful at a variety of levels. Principal G says, "Excursions provide students with additional opportunities to experience the curriculum. As principal, I provide extra support and assistance to staff with instruction and dealing with students with behavioural challenges". There is the need in schools and classrooms to address students' learning and behaviour based on differences in needs rather than equality.

Equality in the educational context or in the classroom means all the learners are treated similarly. They represent similar chronological age and probably the same number of years of formal school. Consequently, decisions are sometimes made to provide these students access to the same curriculum using the same instructional strategies. An assessment of their learning is measured with similar instrument or similar tests. There is limited or no intentional consideration given to differentiation based on cultural context, cognitive ability, motivation, learning styles, linguistic proficiency or economic status. Although there is the recognition of these differences, educators still grapple with the notion of treating each student equally as a sense of fairness.

Managing the perception of fairness and external examination pressures for excellent achievement results on tests such as EQAO, sometimes heighten the tension and anxiety of the classroom teachers. However, great teachers constantly reflect on their practices and their students' achievement and explore new strategies to improve both practice and achievement. It is no wonder that in many classrooms where students demonstrate enhanced academic achievement, teachers seem to be experimenting with equity of opportunities and working towards equity of achievement outcomes. Principals in this sample believed that teachers' focus on equitable practices in PLCs made a difference in the quality of instruction and student achievement. Principal N says, "The overall emphasis on the concept of equity in learning is one of the intangibles that cannot be overstated. At our PLCs we focus on growth mindset and navigating stereotypes". Principal X says, "Equitable practices are evident and observable in each classroom. Teachers play a crucial role as the difference happens in the classrooms. Leadership helps." Jensen (2016) states that the classroom teacher is still the single most significant contributor to student achievement and the effect of the teacher's impact is greater than that of parents, peers, entire schools or poverty (p. 16). However, the same level of achievement is not the reality for all students in all classrooms. Consequently, knowing who the students are and what their needs are should motivate educators to resist any attempt to treat students equally, but intentionally and deliberately demonstrate the use of equitable practices.

Equity means treating each learner differently based on learning needs that are shaped by different experiences resulting in different maturity levels, achievement, self-esteem, motivation, interests among other variables. These differences should not be construed as weaknesses, but as strengths to enhance the richness of the learning experiences for both the teacher and the students. Consequently, if there must be a change in the trajectory of poor academic achievement to high levels of achievement for students from lower socioeconomic backgrounds, our schools and classrooms must portray evidences of a conscious, intentional and focused attempts to use instructional practices that create opportunities for these students to achieve learning outcomes that are based on equitable practices not necessarily equal opportunities.

Blankstein and Noguera (2015) say, "Equity is premised upon a recognition that because all children are different there must be a deep commitment to meet the needs of every child in order to ensure that each student receives what he or she needs to grow and develop and ultimately to succeed" (p. 12). The question therefore is, what constitutes deep commitment and how is it demonstrated in a learning environment? The challenge then is, how to achieve academic success for all students in a diverse classroom restricted by these environmental (postal code or community stigma), sociological (parental education or backgrounds), and psychological (interests and motivation) factors that impact on learning outcomes? From the data collected and analyzed in this study, it is clear that there is diversity in student populations and among the sub-group of learners in the sample schools. If student achievement must be enhanced in these diverse environments, there should be a focus on equity in addressing student learning needs. The high achieving schools in the sample focused on differentiated instructions and CRRP, use of technology and rich questions. All strategies were not implemented in all the schools. However, a combination of the strategies was common practice. The schools have used assessment and demographic data to identify student learning needs and inform pedagogical or instructional practices. As a result, these schools have shown significant student achievement in reading, writing and mathematics according to EQAO results. In these schools, the principals and teachers have used PLCs as the vehicle to develop teacher collaboration, leadership and instructional practices that emphasize equity.

Evidence from the literature indicates that strong leadership emphasizing academic achievement that is supported by individualized instruction, close monitoring and review of students, learning outcomes is a contributing factor. Some elements that characterize this strong leadership include school wide staff development focused on curriculum implementation (Quinn, 2002: Livingston and Schwartz, 2000; Kitchen, DePree, Celedon-Pattichis and Brinkerhoff, 2004). It would seem that there is an inter-relationship among instructional practice, leadership, and professional learning communities (PLC). This inter-relationship connotes the development of expertise in the delivery of instruction. If the emphasis is to meet the diverse learning of all students, then a concerted effort in the pursuit of added knowledge, the exploration of diverse strategies and the focusing of all human and material resources on student learning should be carefully researched and documented.

Goodwin (2011) states that setting high expectations and delivering challenging instruction, are factors that have powerful influence on student achievement. While these factors are perceived as influential, the emphasis should be on pursuing these practices in an attempt to meeting students' learning needs. A true demonstration of high expectations in terms of rich learning activities that trigger higher thinking and create opportunities for learners to use existing knowledge to create new knowledge, flexible and multiple learning strategies that meet diverse learning styles and differentiated assessment practices should be the reality of each student in each classroom.

Research studies on the impact of leadership on student learning have found that leadership is the second most important school-related variable impacting student achievement (Leithwood, Louis, Anderson, and Wahlstrom, 2004). These researchers feel that the effects of leadership on student learning account for a quarter of the total school effects. Also, Ervay (2006) claims, "Academic leadership has always been important because a teacher's success is contingent on the professional culture in which he or she works, one that either encourages or discourages professional and scholastic growth" (p.78). There is a strong belief that this model of leadership practice recognizes and develops staff leadership capacity through collaboration in planning and implementing reflective professional development opportunities that are based on identified student learning needs and aimed at improving teaching and learning.

Louis and Marks (1996) in examining the relationship between the quality of professional collaboration and the quality of classroom pedagogy and student achievement found that achievement level is significantly higher to the extent that schools are strong professional learning communities. Vescio, Ross and Adams (2008) say, "Participation in learning communities impacts teaching practice as teachers become more student centred. In addition, teaching culture is improved because the learning communities increase collaboration, focus on student learning, teacher authority or empowerment, and continuous learning, finally, when teachers participate in a learning community, students benefit as well, as indicated by improved achievement scores over time" (p. 88).

Professional development and professional learning communities (PLCs) have potential to be transformative, in that, individual and school-wide growth is highly probably; teamwork and instructional capacity building resulting in enhanced student academic achievement can be accomplished. Consequently, there is a belief that students from poor communities can achieve at high levels in a school where leadership and instructional practices are catapulted from great to excellent. In this context, all efforts and resources are focused on the development of the entire team and not just a few individuals. It is therefore imperative that school leadership includes teacher leadership capacity building.

Equity Initiatives: Disparities and Persistent Needs

The sample schools in my doctoral dissertation are part of The Toronto District School Board (TDSB) in Ontario. Ontario serves a very diverse student population. Schools in the province are encouraged to celebrate and value the diversity of students' ethnicities, identities, cultures, histories, experiences, races and sexual orientations. Both the Canadian Multiculturalism Act (1971) and Canadian Charter of Rights and Freedoms (1988) mandate the recognition and celebration of these differences. These differences should not be perceived as divisive and negative, but inclusive and positive. Diversity is one of the strengths students bring to the learning environment and to each learning task. These differences must be capitalized on if academic achievement must be maximized. Consequently, the issue of equity of access, inclusion and achievement in education in Canada and more specifically Ontario has resulted in conversations, task forces, inquiries, reports, research studies and policy changes. These strategies have at their core, the improvement of academic achievement for all students. The magnitude and complexity of these challenges however, have attracted the attention and resources of government and community alike. Yet, despite the efforts and resources devoted to the attempts at achieving equitable learning outcomes, there is a preponderance of evidence that inequities persist for some groups of students. The Program of International Student Assessment (PISA) tested students' skills and knowledge in Science, mathematics and reading of school systems in 72 countries aimed at providing global benchmark for equality, equity and efficiency. An analysis of the results using the Organization for Economic Cooperation and Development index for economic, social and cultural status revealed students from economically disadvantaged backgrounds and First Nation students achieved below the average of their other Canadian students (OECD, 2015). Another testing and analysis done in 2018 revealed similar results. Also, Toronto District School Board (2011 and 2016) Census data showed that Black, Hispanic and Indigenous students underperformed in EQAO tests in all areas-reading, writing and mathematics. According to EQAO (2017) Ontario students from families earning less than $30,000.00 per year score 20%-30% lower in Grade 3 math, reading and writing tests than families who earn more than $100.000.00 per year. Students from lower socioeconomic backgrounds (SES), with English as a Second Language (ESL), English Language Learners (ELL) and or Special Education needs, performed lower academically than students from more affluent backgrounds. There is also possibility that the achievement level could be much lower if race intersects with another of these variables. For example, black students could over populate special education classes and come from homes with low SES. These students now have more than one variable that could adversely impact on their academic achievement. Black students' underachievement has recently attracted outrage from some community advocates and educators although many governments have aggressively pursuing policy initiatives to close achievement gaps or produce enhanced academic achievement.

The Ontario Human Rights Code (1962) spells out commitments to achieve equal rights and opportunities, and to end discrimination and harassment connected to race, colour, disability among other differences. In 1993, the Education Act was revised through a Policy and Program Memorandum (PPM 119) requiring School Boards to develop policies on Antiracism and Ethnocultural Education (Segeren and Kutsyuruba, 2012). Until 2008, despite changes in provincial governments, this policy advanced strategies to improve achievement for all students. As part of the initiative, literacy and numeracy strategies were introduced in schools from kindergarten to grade 6 in 2004. Attention was placed on focused curriculum with daily emphasis on literacy and numeracy and targeted supports for low-achieving schools.

Low-achieving schools were identified by their performance on EQAO tests and selected for intervention by the ministry of education in collaboration with school boards. One of the expectations is that each selected school would establish a "turnaround team" of principal, teachers and parents with leadership personnel from the ministry of education. This team would develop local initiatives including extensive training and capacity building for teachers and the principal in order to raise the performance of all the students. Additional funding was allocated to each school to support their initiatives and schools demonstrating improvements in reading, writing and mathematics were expected to share their success stories across the school board and province.

There was no consideration given to the demographic composition and community characteristics of the schools and communities. A significant number of these schools were located in economically disadvantaged neighbourhoods and served students adversely impacted by poverty. A strong point of this initiative was the link to professional development for both principal and teachers. The emphasis was on principal teacher collaboration and the development of instructional practices. As a superintendent of education, I had responsibility to provide leadership to many schools during their implementation of this strategy. One of the schools experienced significant improvement in academic achievement and was named "School on the Run" by the Ministry of Education. The story was chronicled and shared province-wide. As a result of the stories and feedback from these turnaround schools, a provincial Literacy and Numeracy Secretariat was established to provide expert coordination of these initiatives and resources and to develop new working relationships between government, districts and schools (Glaze and Campbell, 2007). The Literacy and Numeracy

Strategy included: school district improvement plans and targets, teams to support improvements in literacy and numeracy at regional, district and school levels, support capacity building for leaders and teachers in literacy and numeracy instruction and in advancing equity outcomes through supporting lower performing students.

A major focus of the Secretariats' work was building professional capacity and leadership in order to lead and implement effective instructional practices for all students especially underachieving groups. Two core components the Literacy Numeracy Strategy were professional development and equity outcomes. These components seem to recognize the importance of professional development and equity in the successful implementation of any initiative aimed at improving academic achievement for a diverse group of students. Fifty-one percent (51%) of the teachers in this sample believed that leadership is associated with academic achievement and 57% believed that professional development is associated with academic achievement. Fifty-five percent (55%) of the teachers also perceived PLCs as associated with student academic achievement. Although approximately 50% of the teachers made no such associations, it still can be insinuated that both leadership and professional development are crucial factors to academic achievement. Winks (2017) says, "When our teachers improve, our schools improve and our students' learning experiences and outcomes improve as well" (p.24).

The data collected from principals' interviews also identified the leadership of the principal in collaborating, mentoring and supporting teachers as strategies associated with enhancing instructional practices, consequently, achievement. PLCs were identified as vehicles to improve instructions. The following quotations highlight the belief: "Principals work with teachers to determine instructional focus and set directions. Teachers at this school share their skills. At our PLCs we focus on growth mindset and barriers to student achievement. In our weekly PLCs we share best practices, current trends and practices in education."

The evidence points to both principals and teachers acknowledging the need for leadership and professional development to facilitate continuous learning and growth as well as identifying and removing of barriers in order to enhance achievement. Several Ontario Ministry of Education policy initiatives were implemented aimed at recognizing differences, barriers and their removal in order to create equitable access to learning opportunities consequently improved achievement for all students.

There was support for English Language Learners in form of a practical guide for Ontario educators Grades 1-8 (Ontario Ministry of Education, 2008). Indigenous students: Ontario's First Nations, Métis and Inuit benefitted from Education Policy Framework: Building Bridges to Success for First Nations, Métis and Inuit Students Developing Policies for Self-Identification: Successful Practices from Ontario School Boards' initiatives (Ontario Ministry of Education, 2007). The Truth and Reconciliation Commission (TRC) founded in 2008 requires that a new vision based on commitment to mutual respect an understanding of the harmful impacts of residential schools, the loss of pride and self-respect of Aboriginal people be developed. At the centre of the TRC is the improvement to legislations, policies, resources and supports for Indigenous peoples' education. The required changes include curriculum and teaching to educate all people in Canada about the historical and contemporary experiences and contributions of Indigenous peoples. Indigenous knowledge and ways of knowing should permeate the education systems (TRC 2015). "Education for All" a strategy aimed at supporting students identified as having Special Educational Needs was also initiated. While these changes are welcome and necessary, without leadership and professional development they could be just a paper exercise. Prejudice, biases and discriminatory practices intentionally or intentionally developed and practised for years need training to change. The Report of the Expert Panel on Literacy and Numeracy Instruction for Students with Special Education Needs, Kindergarten to Grade 6. (Ontario Ministry of Education, 2005) and the Essential for Some, Good for All initiative were also attempted (Hargreaves and Braun, 2011; Hargreaves et al, 2018).

The data compiled from The Literacy and Numeracy initiatives indicated increase in reading and mathematics in elementary schools. The average pass rate improved from 55% (2003) to approximately 70%

(2010) in grade 3 reading, writing, and mathematics. Similarly, about 10-12 percentage points were evident in the same subjects in grade six.

The EQAO data collected from the schools in this sample revealed that Schools D, G, H, N and X ranked 33% above the other 25 schools with the most significant level of challenges, but achieved significantly higher performance ranking in reading, writing and mathematics at the grades 3 and 6 levels. School N (ranked number one on the LOI) consistently outperformed the high performing schools in the sample and also outperformed some schools located in affluent communities and serving students from more affluent backgrounds. One strategy that is common to all the high performing schools in this sample is PLCs. The approaches and frequencies of their PLC activities differed from school to school, but in all the schools the focus was on improving instructional practices and student academic achievement. The implication is that teachers' engagement in frequent and focused PLCs impacts the achievement of students from poor communities. If these activities address equity issues and removing the barriers to learning students should benefit.

Two theories that are pertinent to be explored in these professional development opportunities for both leaders and teachers and mirror the strategies they have reportedly employed are the critical race theory (CRT) and critical pedagogy (CP). CRT describes the approach in which students are trained to use strategies to adapt to racist environments and develop strong racial identities (Carter, 20080). Students are empowered by their leaders and teachers to value themselves and their race. The students, in their schools and classrooms feel valued, included; they access learning activities that encourage critical thinking and that expect them to perform tasks with excellence. Students are encouraged to take risks, develop creativity and embrace failure as part of their learning process. Strategies employed by educators to facilitate and create conducive learning environment form part of critical pedagogy.

Critical pedagogy is the use of instructional techniques, such as having students reflect on current inequitable practices such as stereotype, prejudice and discrimination, to challenge these practices, rise above them and demonstrate excellent performances that defy these beliefs and practices (Duncan-Andrade, 2008). Critical pedagogy mirrors and incorporates aspects of the culturally relevant and responsive pedagogy (CRRP).

CRRP is an approach to teaching that acknowledges the diverse backgrounds of the students and their diverse learning needs. This approach capitalizes on cultural knowledge, prior experiences, frame of reference and learning styles of ethnically diverse students to make learning encounters more relevant to them (Gay, 2010). Since the student population in schools is becoming increasingly different in racial, cultural and socioeconomic composition to that of the teaching staff, teachers constantly need to develop the skills, knowledge, and dispositions culturally responsive to and to nurture relationships with their students that empower them to develop academically and socio-politically (Gay, 2003). This approach to instruction, by teachers, values students and the wealth of knowledge and experiences they bring to the classrooms, recognizes these attributes as strengths rather than deficits and incorporates them into practices that are engaging. Engaged students are bound to produce excellent achievement.

From principals' responses to the interview question asking them to describe the student population, demography and strengths, it was deduced that each of the schools was populated with diverse learners who possessed varying degrees of psychological (level of motivation and interest in learning, sociological (familial expectations and level of education) and environmental (students' levels of responsibilities, rich histories and heritage). This implies that the learners represented in these schools maybe similar to other populations not included in this sample, but present in Toronto's schools. Therefore, it can be concluded that the reasons these schools in this sample are making progress at improving academic achievement for economically disadvantaged students is not because of the composition of their population, but maybe through their teaching-learning practices developed in their PLCs. Principals say, "There are 33 different languages present at this school. Students possess strong oral language tradition. Students view school as a positive space. Many students at an early age undertake many responsibilities in their families". Students' strengths are incorporated in the learning environment and valued. When students feel valued and included, they tend to meet or exceed expectations. Principal respondents in this study identified CRRP and differentiated instruction as strategies responsible for the high level of success experienced by their schools serving students from poor communities. Their responses include, "Most teachers use CRRP, have growth mindset, hold high expectations for all students, connect students' histories and experiences to the curriculum and are sensitive to Social Justice issues" Some of the teachers in the sample say, "We believe that the teaching and learning environment should be inclusive and promote the intellectual engagement of all students and should reflect the individual strengths, needs, learning preferences and cultural perspectives of each student". The high performing schools in this sample recognize students' differences, view these differences as strengths and incorporate these differences into the curriculum and teaching and learning strategies. These schools' academic achievement levels are high. What then can other schools learn from their experience?

The evidence from my review of policies, initiatives, school and EQAO data shows improvement in student achievement, narrowing of achievement gap for some sub-groups of learners. However, Blacks, Hispanic and Indigenous students- First Nations Metis and Inuit still lagged behind in their performance. Students from these sub-groups of learners performed at lower level than their counterparts from higher SES backgrounds (TDSB Census Portraits June, 2015). Another key finding from the reviews is the link between leadership and professional development and enhanced academic achievement. The implication is that leadership is important, but also a critical mass of teachers needs to be trained in order to gain maximum impact and sustained efforts. The schools in this sample, D (reading 66%, writing 80% and math 62%), G (reading 90%, writing 85%, math 80%) H (reading 80%, writing 89% and math 61%), N (reading 93%, writing 93% and math 93%) and X (reading 62%, writing 76% and math 73%) show achievement above expectations and reported staffs' engagement in frequent and focused PLCs. This focus could have minimized the fluctuating of results observed in other schools as a result of change in leadership, teachers and cohorts of students. Sometime, when a principal changes school, some teachers take jobs at other schools and even students change classes, there is observable change in the performance of the same cohort of students. The EQAO data for the schools in this sample were collected over three consecutive years. The schools' performance remains consistently high. The implication is that if leadership and professional development efforts are sustained, there is possibility that high levels of academic achievement will be consistently maintained. On the other hand, if teachers do not frequently participate in PLCs, academic achievement maybe low. The focus on equity strategies to improve the quality of instructional practices then should permeate all policy initiatives. Campbell (2017) argues that teacher development in Canada has contributed to relatively high PISA scores and that teaching quality and professional learning will be critical for supporting low SES children in the future. Currently, the call from advocates for school boards to eliminate anti-black racism is more pronounced. The impact of the inter-connection between race and SES on academic achievement must be acknowledged. Strategies must be implemented to remove any barriers that students with these designations face. All educators need constant training and development if they are to make needed changes to student achievement. One of the strategies to change the trajectory of low achievement to high achievement seems to be professional learning communities (PLCs).

CHAPTER THREE

TRANSFORMATIVE LEADERSHIP

The multiplicity and complexity that characterize the leadership role of schools have kept the topic as a focus in the literature and research for decades. The renewed call for accountability that expects each school to produce outstanding academic achievement for all students has resulted in researchers' differentiating aspects of the leadership function or role, presenting various iterations and definitions of leadership and careful analyses of leadership application in school improvement and student achievement. In addition to the definitions and application of the roles, there are also definitions of leadership styles and research studies on their impact on organizational performance. Leadership style highlights the characteristics and behaviours used by leaders to interact with their subordinates (Mitonga-Monga andCoetzee, 2012). Some of the well researches leadership styles include: charismatic (Germano, 2010), democratic (Bhargavi and Yaseen, 2016), autocratic (Iqbal, Anwar and Haider, 2015), bureaucratic (Germano, 2010), transformational (Jyoti and Bhau, 2015) and transformative (Collins, Bruce and McKee, 2019). This researcher is aware that a leader may demonstrate more predominantly a particular leadership style or may even use a multiplicity of styles based on situational variables. For example, while the democratic style maybe preferred, the leader may need to make an executive decision in a time sensitive situation and uses what maybe perceived as an autocratic style. However, despite the perceived inherent strengths in each style and the benefits to organizational performance, this dissertation focuses on the transformative leadership style.

Transformative leadership focuses on systemic changes and interrogates questions of justice and democracy; it critiques inequitable practices and offers promise of greater achievement and a better way of life (Shields, 2010). Through this leadership style equity and justice can be enhanced. In the school context, academic achievement for marginalized learners can be improved consequently, their life chances. Another strength of transformative leadership is the recognition that leadership exists at all echelons of the school. Therefore, drawing on the leadership of the teachers is a crucial and necessary element in any improvement effort and process. Transformative leadership views improvement as a process. This implies that student achievement is never complete, but a work in progress. One level of accomplishment triggers a higher level of success, greater efforts and resilience on the part of the leaders and students alike. Both transformative leadership and equity then are mutually inclusive. As a result, transformative leadership should characterize the roles and behaviours of those who undertake responsibilities for enhanced achievement for students. From the principals' responses to the interview questions, it is deduced that all the schools in the sample focus on a social justice process. Principal X says, "Leaders and teachers develop and use a social justice kit". Principal D says, "Leaders and teachers focus on social justice issues in implementing curriculum and assessment practices". The implication is that there is a recognition and use of transformative leadership connected to social justice aimed at higher academic achievement.

It must be acknowledged that in a climate of complexities and challenges, there are many areas of effective school operation that compete for the attention and efforts of both administrators and teachers. However, if schools are to effectively accomplish the goal for which they have been established-- student achievement, then leadership must be the centre of their core business. Van de Grift and Houtveen (1999) define leadership as principals' ability to initiate school improvement, create a learning oriented educational climate and stimulate and supervise teachers in ways that maximize the effectiveness of their tasks. Leadership has also been described as, "Having a clear vision of instructional excellence and continuous professional development consistent with the goal of the improvement of teaching and learning" (Hoy and Hoy, 2003, p.2). Additionally, Edmonds (1979) asserts that principals with backgrounds as strong classroom instructors provide instructional practices and leadership by using their knowledge and experience to develop curriculum, provide professional development opportunities, monitor the implementation and effectiveness and develop a positive school culture. The teachers in this sample perceived with a median score of 51% that leadership is associated with student academic achievement. Also, from the data, at 0.01 level of significance, leadership is correlated with instruction (variance 0.914), professional development (variance 0.907) and professional learning communities (variance 0.910). There is an overall correlation with leadership and the other variables at (variance 0.972). From the data, instructional practices, leadership, professional development and professional learning communities show significantly high levels of correlation. These significant correlations imply that a high level of student academic achievement is dependent on a synergy of the variables. Put another way, the more of the variables on which there is strong leadership, the higher the achievement level that the school will experience. All the schools in the sample identified significantly high correlation with instructional practices and have demonstrated high academic achievement.

The significant correlations between leadership, professional learning communities (PLCs) imply that when leadership implements and supports staff participation in professional development opportunities, there is possibility that expertise will be developed. The expertise developed by staff has propensity to impact student academic achievement. On the contrary, lack of effective leadership and participation in professional learning may lead to student underachievement.

While the definitions speak clearly to the principals' ability, vision and background to provide leadership, there is also the insinuation of teacher leadership through professional development opportunities.

DuFour et. al. (2005) state, "Principals in PLCs are called upon to regard themselves as leaders of leaders rather than leaders of followers, and broadening teacher leadership becomes one of their priorities" (p.23). Also, Marks and Printy (2003) in highlighting the shift in thinking of principals as leaders with sole expertise in curriculum, instruction and assessment practices, assert that teachers are the rightful instructional leaders in the building. There needs to be the recognition of teacher expertise and leadership and a conscious effort to utilize these skills to achieve better learning outcomes. The individuals occupying the elm of formal leadership and tasked with the responsibilities of student achievement must be aware of their strengths in the area, but also be willing to delegate responsibilities to teachers with more expertise. This delegation of responsibilities should not reflect a hands-off approach, but mirror an authentic learning stance-- administrators and teachers learning together. This approach requires vulnerability on the part of all involved and can only truly be accomplished in an atmosphere of trust. As people develop trust, their comfort level to honestly articulate their strengths and weaknesses without fear of judgment is heightened.

Involvement in curriculum, instruction and assessment is considered critical to the concept of leadership (Marzano et al, 2005; Stein and D'Amico, 2000) in underscoring the importance of this responsibility in the principal-ship, also state that knowledge of subject matter and pedagogy should be as important to administrators as it is to teachers. Fullan (2001) highlights the importance of this responsibility by explaining that the principal's knowledge of effective practices in curriculum, instruction and assessment is necessary to provide guidance for teachers on the day-to-day tasks of teaching and learning. Elmore (2000) also says, "Leadership is the guidance and direction of instructional improvement" (p.13). Again, one is cognizant that all knowledge and expertise are not resident in the principals, but equally talented teachers. A collaboration of both teacher and principal knowledge and expertise should significantly benefit students.

According to Hallinger (2003) a theory of leadership has the following components: a climate of high expectations and educational innovations and improvement, a shared sense of purpose in the school, a reward structure that reflects the school's mission and goals for staff and students, a variety of activities designed to intellectually stimulate the faculty and staff and continuous professional development for them and pedagogical knowledge and skills. These leadership qualities align with the transformative leadership style and Dweck's (2006) concept of growth mindset. The growth mindset exposes the idea that abilities can be developed through commitment, dedication and hard work. This point of view encourages learning and resilience as attributes of achieving excellence. Principals, teachers and students must recognize their ability to contribute to the necessary changes and work together on an established path to achieve stated outcomes. On this journey, all participants should review progress, demonstrate creativity and flexibility in making needed changes. Principals in response to the interview questions attributed the success of their schools to teacher and principal collaboration. They further explained the collaborative process to mean the empowerment of teachers to co-lead with administrators to plan and implement professional development opportunities. Principal N says, "The key to the success of this school is the team approach to building instructional capacity. Teachers work in collaboration with administrators to develop understanding and address students' learning needs". Principal H in describing teachers' impact on students' academic achievement says, "The success of the school is achieved because of teacher efficacy and collaboration. Teacher efficacy and collaboration are key to student success."

The theory purported includes elements that should contribute to the effectiveness of the school organization, pedagogical knowledge and skills. This theory constitutes one of the key functions for which our schools have been established. Therefore, if schools are to be effective in the pursuit of this very important goal- improving achievement for all students, all efforts and resources must be directed to this accomplishment. This however, should not be seen as a prescription, but rather suggestions of possibilities. The unique needs of each school should be the determinant factors in the choices made and focus determined.

Marks and Printy (op. cit.) state that effective principals model leadership behaviours and invite teachers to participate. The principal, therefore, in understanding his or her responsibilities, can contribute to the building of teaching and learning capacity. Hattie (2012) says, "Improvements relate to building a collective capacity of teachers in a school to show success- not only in achievement, but also in making learning a valued outcome, by retaining students' interest in learning, in making students respect themselves and others, by recognizing and esteeming diversity" (p.150). Principals in the sample opine that principals must provide administrative support to teachers and work collaboratively with them to improve instruction. In doing so, according to the principals, they not only demonstrate well-rounded leadership, but exhibit an openness and willingness to be mentored and to learn from others. Principal N says, "Principal demonstrates leadership that is well rounded and be mentored by other leaders who are". Principal G comments, "As a principal, I work with teachers to determine instructional focus and set direction". Principal D says, "Teachers feel supported by administrators". Hattie (ibid.) further recommends that schools develop a collective agreement on key knowledge, skills and disposition to be learned, strategies to determine the impact of teaching on student learning, the identification of students and the provision of multiple opportunities to learn and demonstrate learning, share errors, successes and consistent passion for teaching. While the principal can contribute and provide guidance and direction in this very important work, the overall school performance rests on the collective efforts and leadership of the teachers as well.

Ylimaki (2007) in a study of four diverse high poverty schools found that there were differences in leadership. Two of the schools experienced significant improvement in student achievement. He concluded that schools with more effective leadership demonstrate the ability to delegate leadership. The teachers were therefore committed to and felt responsible for student success and failures. Johnson, Livingston and Schwartz (2000) suggest that the leadership of the principal directly affects student learning by influencing academic expectations and opportunities for learning and instructional organization. Some teachers in the sample say, "Our principals developed teachers' leadership skills and knowledge in the planning and designing of school-based professional development. The principal and teacher leaders work collaboratively on professional development opportunities aimed at impacting teaching and learning in our school." Some of the principal respondents also identified, " teacher empowerment to take lead" as a professional development strategy used to support teachers implementing teaching-learning initiatives to support students living in poverty.

From the preponderance of evidence in the research studies (Steiner, and Kowal, (2007; Leithwood, and Seashore-Louis, 2011; Robinson, 2011) and from the data collected and analyzed in this study, it is clear that the leadership of the principal plays a critical and crucial role in developing teacher collaboration, instructional capacity, leadership and consequently, effectiveness. The quality of the leadership impacts on teacher expertise on instruction, curriculum, assessment and the provision of data-based intervention and opportunities that facilitate academic achievement. Fullan (2001) advises school leaders that there are no magic solutions to making schools successful. Fifty-one (51%) of the teachers in this sample believed that leadership is associated with academic achievement and that effective principals work in collaboration with staff to set expectations and success criteria for high level of student achievement, agree on the quality of learning outcomes and strategies to monitor progress. Also, there was the belief that these principals create the environment for teachers to willingly seek support in developing expertise. They value the importance of empowering others and sharing of responsibilities. The principals in the sample believed that leadership contributed to their schools' success. Principals H in highlighting leadership contribution to students' academic achievement says, "Principals lead by example and demonstrate flexibility to accommodate the needs and expertise of their staff in scheduling classes and deciding on teaching assignments". Principal H says, "In PLCs, principals provide coaching support to teachers. We are in the trenches with our teachers. We frequently participate in co-planning and co-teaching". Principal G says, "In co-planning and co-teaching, we facilitate the use of data in monitoring student progress. Teachers in teams recognize and share expertise and create opportunities for problem-solving on meeting students' learning needs." From the data collected from the principals' responses to their interviews, it is deduced that principals facilitated collaborative professional learning and worked closely with teachers to develop instructional practices to enhance teaching and learning. The principals perceived that sustained collaborative professional development impacts on students' learning goals and more specifically benefits their students from poor communities.

By extension, there is no magic wand to enhance academic achievement. However, effective leadership that facilitates creative, consistent and meaningful professional development informed by data on learning needs will build teacher efficacy and spread the instructional "wealth" to all classrooms to benefit all students, especially those from poor communities. Put another way, leadership of the principal influences teacher instructional practices which in turn influence students' academic achievement. Professional learning communities are vehicles to enhance the level of impact or influence. It therefore takes concerted efforts on the part of all those who are in trusted the responsibilities to educate students to recognize the students' diversity, explore and utilize a multiplicity of resources and strategies to improve their achievement.

As schools continue to face community pressure to improve academic achievement, leaders must focus their attention and efforts on demonstrating the belief that all students can learn and achieve success. Stronge, Richard and Catano (2008) argue that principals should concentrate on building a vision for their schools, sharing leadership with teachers and influencing schools to operate as learning communities. Also, Reason and Reason (2007) believe that as leaders, principals share their leadership with teachers to improve reflection and collaborative investigation to improve teaching and learning. Subsequently, teacher leaders lead change from the classroom by asking questions related to improvement and they feel empowered to help find answers.

Principals, therefore, in order to achieve learning for all students, should undertake their responsibility by developing and encouraging an environment of mutual trust that challenges teachers' pedagogical practices, encourages creative risk taking and provides support to engage transformational and sustainable teaching and learning. In this environment, shared leadership and continuous learning are encouraged, teacher collaboration is evident and intentional and focused opportunities are provided for principals and teachers to co-lead and co-learn. Hargreaves and Frank (2003) purport that principals who use distributive leadership practice across their schools may experience sustainable improvements within the school organization. Consequently, principals need to draw on the expertise of teacher leaders in their schools in order to enhance improvement efforts and results (Mark and Printy, 2003).

An organizational framework that facilitates shared or distributive leadership is described in the literature as "collaborative inquiry" (CI) – an approach that empowers teachers to take full responsibility for their professional learning informed by evidence generated from the triangulation of both qualitative and quantitative data. It must be noted that both shared and distributive leadership is used interchangeably to describe the practice of mobilizing and empowering individuals to take leadership in areas of their expertise. This includes encouraging teachers to provide leadership to various initiatives such as PLC. The data sources should include student achievement, but even more importantly, student demographic data- socioeconomic (family income below, Low Income Measure, families receiving social assistance, lone parent families and adults level of educational attainment). The careful analysis of multiple data sources has the potential to provide rich information on diverse perspective on a common issue or challenge to be explored.

National and international studies highlight both the characteristics and benefits of collaborative inquiry. *Figure 3.1 provides an overview.

* (Timperlay, Kaser and Halbert, 2014; Comber, 2013, Hannay, Wideman and Seller, 2010)

Figure 3.1 Organizing Framework for Collaborative Inquiry Process

Ministry of Education: Capacity building Series, September, 2014

The diagram postulates: student engagement and learning in the classroom should be the focus of professional learning and collaborative inquiry; professional discourse should generate new knowledge and serve as catalyst to refine practice and educators build pedagogical content knowledge for their own practice.

A culture of inclusivity must be part of collaborative inquiry mindset when interpreting evidence and studying the students' experiences. This approach points to a careful analysis of multiple data sources- qualitative, quantitative and perceptual data (participants' perception, attitudes and feelings) of student learning needs and experiences as the core and fundamental premise for educators' professional development. To be relevant and transformative, any such professional development opportunity must reflect students' learning and any gap in pedagogical practices that would present barriers to each learner maximizing his or her potentials. Leaders, therefore, must undertake their responsibility for student enhanced academic achievement with a mindset of equity, inclusivity and excellence for all students. The strategy to achieve this very important, relevant and urgent educational goal is collaboration demonstrated by all the practitioners involved in effecting student learning outcomes.

A review of the literature points to the extensive benefits to be accrued from teacher collaboration. Curtis and City (2010) view teacher collaboration and teamwork as peripheral to improving instructional quality and learning for all students. They claim that when teams functioning effectively in a system, it has tremendous implications for the system to organize and focus on instructional improvement. Teacher collaboration has potential to enhance learning opportunities. In schools where this collaboration occurs, students benefit and achievement stands a chance of improving.

The emphasis on program coherence, consistency of expectations should be paralleled with coherence and consistency of excellent instructional practices. The complexities involved in allowing each student to reach her maximum learning potentials regardless of systemic barriers, changes in curricular expectations, teacher training and frequent changes in teaching personnel, cannot be the sole responsibility of just an individual teacher, but on the collective team effort of all the teachers. This speaks to the identification of the mutual core purpose--- educating every child with a mindset that this purpose is achievable and a successful outcome is dependent on shared expertise. Inger (1993) identifies the following benefits that can be achieved from teacher collaboration: teacher leadership through formal and informal training sessions, study groups, and conversations about teaching, teachers and administrators get the opportunities to get smarter together; teachers are better prepared to support one another's strengths and accommodate weaknesses; working together, they reduce their individual planning time while greatly increasing the available pool of ideas and materials; schools become better prepared and organized to examine new ideas, methods and materials; the staffs become adaptable and self-reliant; teachers are organized to ease the strain of staff turnover, both by providing systemic professional assistance to beginners and by explicitly socializing all new comers, including veteran teachers, to staff values, traditions and resources (p. 11).

Since there is a preponderance of evidence from the research that both teacher collaboration and professional learning communities (PLCs) lead to improved student achievement and that shared leadership is instrumental in their development, the challenge then, is how to develop and maintain collaboration at each school level. The National Association of Elementary Schools Principals (NAESP) (2002) recommends some standards for consideration: balanced management and leadership roles, high expectations and standards, culture of adult learning, use multiple sources of data as diagnostic tools, actively engaged community and demand content and instruction that ensure achievement.

The standards for consideration connote that principals prioritize between the managerial aspects of their role (attendance monitoring, facility repairs, routine organizational practices and procedures among others) and the leadership roles (initiating and implementing new curricular offerings, pedagogy and staff development strategies). The leadership aspect of the role should also not only establish high expectations, but create the atmosphere for all adults in the building and beyond to develop expertise and partnerships to rise to the challenges of meeting the high expectations. To achieve high expectations therefore, there should not only be a demand on curricular content and instruction, but a careful study and agreement on which approach and strategies should be implemented and why. The achievement of this goal will require all educators tasked with attaining student achievement to collaborate on their efforts. A test to the principal's leadership is the propensity to deal with ambiguity, manage distractions and keep the focus on teaching and learning in spite of seemingly important activities competing for attention, efforts and resources.

Leadership, therefore, is crucial to any success in implementing these recommended standards. The NAESP (op.cit.) article in differentiating between management and leadership roles, further states that principals engaged in creating a culture of adult learning will: provide time for reflection as an important part of improving practice, invest in teacher learning, connect professional development to school learning goals, provide opportunities for teachers to work, plan and think together and recognize the need to continually improve principals' own professional practice (p. 42).

The more principals and teachers collaborate, share leadership responsibilities and learning continually together, an approach described by Senge (1992) as the learning organization and aligns with the concept of the learning leader (Reeves, 2006), the more achievement is enhanced. In this environment, relationships based on mutual trust, principal trusting teachers, teachers trusting principals and teachers trusting other teachers, should permeate all operations and activities. This atmosphere makes it possible for all participants to be vulnerable without being judged, risk taking and creativity to surface, diverse beliefs to be articulated and challenged, collective will strengthened and new strategies explored, finalized and pursued. The incidental learning of collaboration and leadership development mirrored from this practice, sometimes out-weigh the planned expectations. The greatest benefit of this organizational improvement however, is that principals and teachers become better, learning together.

According to Senge (op. cit.), the learning organization is predicated on the following dimensions: system thinking- understanding of the whole as well as the component parts and personal mastery- individual strives to enhance his vision and focuses his energy and be in a constant state of learning. Learning organization also embraces a mental model- recognizing ingrained assumptions and generalizations and challenging these assumptions to allow for new ideas and changes. These organizations build shared vision- to influence and motivate behaviour change through dialogue, commitment and enthusiasm and team learning. Team members think together to achieve common goals.

The collaborative nature implicit in these dimensions means that both principals and teacher leaders must undertake responsibilities to create the environment and culture that make improvement of student learning the hallmark of the school's operation. In this environment, new evidence-based teaching strategies can be explored and implemented. The culture can then truly reflect capacity building or the development of collective expertise.

In today's complex and diverse school environment, it is inconceivable to envision leadership as totally resident in the principalship. There must be an acknowledgement that in effective schools, the principal's role is significant in school improvement- developing a collaborative plan informed by a multiplicity of data sources identifying student learning needs, strategies for instruction and monitoring, and strategies for instructional capacity building. However, if there is ever going to be large scale, systemic, transformational and sustainable changes and improvement to student learning and academic achievement, there must be an intentional attempt at recognizing and developing leadership at all echelons of the school organization. Individuals in formal leadership positions such as principals must therefore recognize the expertise and potentials of teachers and draw on these valuable resources to enhance learning and achievement. Katzenmeyer and Moller (2001) say, "When given opportunities to lead, teachers can influence school reform efforts. Waking this sleeping giant of teacher leadership has unlimited potential in making a real difference in the pace and depth of school change" (p.102).

The concept of "teacher leadership" is not a new phenomenon. However, there is very little consensus on its definition and application. The general agreement is that teacher leadership involves more than individuals with formal roles and responsibilities. This group includes teachers without direct responsibility for teacher evaluation; teachers in this group have a significant amount of trust among peers, possesses a propensity to influence and mobilize others on a common purpose such as improving academic achievement for economically disadvantaged students. The group also demonstrates observable evidence of commitment to student learning and a willingness to share resources and expertise in a non-judgemental atmosphere. The key to the success of this leadership role is the trust ascribed to this informal position by peers.

Harris and Muijs (2015) in a paper titled, Teacher Leadership: Principles and Practices, express the point of view that teacher leadership is primarily concerned with developing high quality learning and teaching with a core focus upon improving learning on a premise of professional collaboration, development and growth. They believe that teacher leadership incorporates: the leadership of other teachers through coaching, mentoring, leading work groups, the leadership of developmental tasks that are central to improved learning and teaching and the leadership of pedagogy through the development and modeling of effective forms of teaching (p.2).

While these activities portray teachers in leadership roles, teachers' efforts and operations must be in alignment with administrative leadership and implemented within the framework of collaboration. In a shared leadership school environment therefore, there is empowerment, risk-taking, new initiatives and flexibility in approach to producing high levels of achievement outcomes. In this atmosphere of collaboration, there is greater probability that the learning needs of students living in poverty will be addressed and achieved. Regardless of the definition ascribed to teacher leadership or even the configuration of this group of leaders, this concept acknowledges that the effectiveness of any instructional practices, consequently, student academic achievement, rests with teachers.

From a review of the literature, York-Bar and Duke (2004) point to the concept where formal administrative leadership roles augments teacher expertise and vice versa:

> Recognition of teacher leadership stems in part from
> new understandings about organizational development
> and leadership that suggest active involvement by
> individuals at all levels and within all domains of an

organization is necessary if change is to take hold......
Educational improvement at the level of instruction, for
example, necessarily involves leadership by teachers in
classrooms and with peers (p. 255).

There seems to be the recognition that improvement in instruction
is inextricably linked to teacher involvement and leadership. This can be
likened to a "grass-root movement" or what is described in the literature
as leadership from the bottom or from the middle (Fullan, 2015).
However, in spite of the characterization or definition, there is a strong
belief that teacher leadership supports effective school improvement.
Successful school improvement includes academic achievement for all.
Harris and Muijs (2003) identified the benefits of teacher leadership as:
improving school effectiveness, teacher effectiveness and contributing
to school improvement. Also, Lieberman, Saxl and Miles (1988) opine
that teacher leaders have a strong sense of purpose, develop collegial
relationships and collaboration, move beyond the boundaries of their
classrooms and influence colleagues without the use of overt power.

These qualities of teacher leaders are in alignment with Jackson's
et.al. (2010) view. They believe that teacher leaders positively impact
on work ethic, teamwork, leadership, openness, vision, positive effects,
risk-taking and teaching related skills. Principal N says, "Staff work
incredibly well together. They work in grade teams and even have
lunch as a group". Principal D says, "Teachers at this school share
their skills". Principal X says, "Teachers work in collaboration with
one another to improve instruction". From both the data analysis in
this study and the literature review, it can be gleaned that at the heart
of school improvement then, is teacher leadership. This leadership
contributes to team work, collaboration and instructional capacity
building. These contributing factors are key components to enhance
academic achievement for all learners, not just a few. In classrooms and
schools where these factors are evident, and the practice of developing
instructional skills collaboratively become common, intentional and
focused practice, student learning outcome must be improved. These
classrooms and schools can boast maximum impact achieved through

shared expertise development rather than individualized expertise in only one classroom.

In a column in Association for Supervision and Curriculum Development (ASCD) Express, Ben Fenton in an article titled, "New Leaders for New Schools: Forming Aligned Instructional Leadership Teams" (2016), writes:

> Principals cannot lead schools to make break-through achievement gains on their own: the support of an aligned instructional leadership team is crucial. Depending on the strengths and the job design of individuals in the school, the aligned instructional leadership team may include teacher leaders, instructional coaches, and assistant principals. Leadership team members are responsible for implementing school wide initiatives for instruction, and they also model cultural norms. So, it's imperative that the members of the leadership team share the vision of the school (p.1).

The writer implies teacher leadership, collaboration, influence and capacity building as important attributes to a shared vision. Identifying, building and utilizing teacher expertise or strength is crucial to the development of shared leadership and foundational to learning for all students. Hattie (2012) identifies some major dimensions of teacher expertise as: high level of knowledge and understanding of subject matter, guiding learning to describable and deep outcomes, successfully monitoring learning and providing feedback that assists students to progress, attending to the more attitudinal attributes of learning and providing defensible evidence of positive impacts of teaching and on student learning. He further expands on the concept of "teacher expert" to include the teacher's integration of subject knowledge with students' prior knowledge and the modifying of each lesson according to students' learning needs. This, of course, includes students who live in poverty and may even come to the learning tasks with gaps in their prior achievement. This approach to learning should be evident in all classrooms, should characterize the instructional practices of all teacher leaders who would then ignite the flames of learning for all and expand the influence in all classrooms and schools. Put another way, systemic high academic achievement for all students cannot be fully realized by individual principal serving as instructional leader in one school, but by all principals in all schools and expert teachers in all classrooms.

Darrielson (2006) postulates a framework for teacher leadership that aligns to this current stance or position. The framework depicts student learning at the centre, but extends teaching and learning beyond department to teams, across school and beyond school. This model of teacher leadership influence, points to the direction of successful learning outcomes for all students especially for those from economically disadvantaged backgrounds. If educational endeavours must realize their goal, that of maximizing student academic achievement for students from poor communities, a renewed look at professional learning communities and the authentic learning opportunities possible through this approach to teacher leadership capacity building, is a direction that must be pursued. In schools where leadership and accountability for high academic achievement extends beyond the main office to individual classrooms, there exists greater possibilities of improved learning outcomes.

Fullan (2007) reviewed a number of research studies and identified some findings he classified as "known" about teacher effectiveness. Teachers strong on content and pedagogical knowledge, and who care deeply, have moral purpose about learning and students. Teachers who are internal (assessment for learning) and external (assessment of learning) use data on an ongoing basis for both improving learning and making progress. Teachers who learn from others (again, on an ongoing basis) inside and outside of the classroom and are led by principals and other school leaders who foster the first three qualities. Also, teachers in districts that focus on developing district-wide cultures, develop and cultivate the previous four elements. The teachers in state systems that integrate accountability and capacity building while establishing partnerships across the three levels: school, community and district develop teaching expertise together (p.1).

The highlights focus laser light on some of the essential and key components that should be evident in all classrooms and schools. Among these key components of effectiveness is the teacher leader "power of knowing"– knowing content, pedagogy and the learners. The expansion of this knowledge extends beyond classroom assessment data to include demographic information on family income, level of education and family composition. These variables do have significant ramifications for teaching and learning outcomes. Conversely, teaching with the absence of this knowledge can lead to unsuccessful learning outcomes for students from economically deprived environments. Another key factor is that teacher leader not only recognizes his or her level of expertise or competence, but also knows where there are gaps and is willing to learn from others. This power of knowing therefore has the propensity for capacity building and expansion of teacher effectiveness, leadership and collaboration. The beneficiaries of an approach that inculcates these criteria widely implemented are the diverse student populations our schools serve. Erkens (2008) concludes that if teachers are to lead from the classroom in a manner that impacts on student learning in significant ways, they must be collaborators, action researchers, reflective practitioners and learner advocates. Danielson (2006) in identifying what teacher leaders do, includes using evidence and data in decision-making, mobilizing people around a common purpose, monitoring progress and adjusting the approach as conditions change, contributing to a learning organization and a deep commitment to student learning. While there are similar threads in agreements on the findings and criteria, the difference is in the varying degrees of commitment and implementation in a school, among schools, across a system and across systems. The challenge we face is how to achieve consistent and effective practices to benefit all learners. The answer seems to reside in effective teacher leadership developed in professional development communities (PLCs). Principal D says, "Teachers in this school are encouraged to take leadership in planning and leading staff PLCs". Principal N says, "Teachers come to the learning environment with different levels of expertise. Teachers share resources and success stories with one another". These quotations reflect the principals' beliefs in teacher leadership in relationship to PLCs. The responses also imply the need for teacher leadership in improving instructional practices to benefit the students.

One caution, however, is prudent. This directional approach will not be successful in a vacuum, but must be implemented alongside other variables such as "school community relationships" that has a positive correlation to enhanced student academic achievement. Leithwood (2010) claims that 50% of the variables that impact on student achievement occur in the classrooms, that includes teaching and learning. This study attempts to discover some of these variables that probably have direct influence on student academic achievement. The hope is to be able to offer possible strategies to maximize academic achievement.

Since there is evidence that links teacher leadership to student academic achievement, the logical conclusion then, is high performing schools and by extension systems, need to invest in the development of teacher leadership or expertise. Fullan and Hargreaves (2012) described this phenomenon as professional capital and indicated that when the vast majority of teachers possess the power of professional capital, they become smart and talented, committed and collegial, thoughtful and wise. They concluded that these teachers' moral purpose is expressed in their relentless, expert-driven pursuit of serving their students and their communities and are always learning how to do better. A full demonstration of talents, commitment, collegiality maybe the needed application our schools need to improve learning not for just some students but for all.

This pursuit, therefore, must be connected to the belief that all students have the inherent ability to achieve success and that the communities in which they live may limit the success, but do not determine the level or finality of these students' success. Consequently, all schools, in the pursuit of their core mandate---high academic achievement for all learners, must invest time, resources and leadership in providing professional development opportunities to their teaching staff. There is a strong belief that their investment will produce the fruits of improved academic achievement. York-Barr and Duke (2004) believe that congruency between a school's mission and the teachers' values results in greater participation in curricular, instructional and assessment goals which also leads to acceptance of varying levels of leadership responsibility, commitment to on-going professional development and sustainable changes in improved educational practice to benefit all students. The challenge is how to make this core mandate an achievable goal in all of our schools. Schools are faced with high teacher turnover, limited budget, safety and security issues, sometime, transient student population, issues of poverty, very diverse learners and the pressure to achieve high levels of academic learning outcomes.

Katzenmeyer and Moller (2001) offer the following suggestions: shorten faculty meetings with less administrative procedures and announcements, require professional growth plans instead of annual evaluations, provide on-going professional development throughout the school year and beyond, cover classes using administrators and volunteers to free up teachers to meet, collaborate and plan, pool classes of students occasionally to free up teachers to meet and plan, engage students in community service projects and learning activities to facilitate teacher collaboration schedule common planning periods by grade level or content area and extend instruction on four days and reduce on one day.

However, one caution is prudent. These suggestions can only be experimented with the agreement of teachers and their union. Principals, nevertheless, may capitalize on the elements of these suggestions and other creative strategies to empower teachers to undertake leadership, build collaboration and relationships. An emphasis in this area has potential to build highly sustained teacher expertise to enhance teaching and learning. The end game is that students will be exposed to high quality teaching that meets their learning needs in all classrooms. Therefore, a school's academic achievement cannot only be attributed to what students bring or did not bring to the learning tasks and environment, but on the quality of the teaching and learning opportunities afforded students in their learning pursuit. Lieberman and Friedrich (2010) believe that teacher leadership is best developed through the demonstration of best practices in curriculum, instruction and assessment, understanding of the school culture, initiation and support of change and the development of colleagues in a variety of settings. Also, Birky, Shelton and Headley (2006) opine that teacher leaders potentially can lead their colleagues to optimal performance levels based on a shared commitment to student learning, empowerment, relationships and collaboration. Principal H says, "I empower my teachers to take responsibilities for planning and leading PLCs. Teachers share strategies and success stories with one another. I work with teachers to share best practices in PLCs". Principal G says, "At our PLCs we focus on understanding and eliminating barriers to student achievement". Principal X says, "We study various data and use the information to decide on students' levels of achievement". Principal H says, "At our weekly PLCs we share best practices, current trends and practices in education. We use learning buddies to provide professional development for other teachers. Teacher leaders use collaborative inquiry to do research and guide their practice". These qualities consistently exhibited by any school should result in high level of student achievement for all learners especially, our most vulnerable learners from economically disadvantaged communities. The hope is that principals and teachers participating in professional learning communities (PLCs) will result in a difference in what schools do for students.

CHAPTER FOUR

PROFESSIONAL LEARNING COMMUNITIES (PLCS): A WAY FORWARD

Professional Learning Community is an educational concept that has undergone many decades of research and practice and consequently, revision. However, it still remains a construct that varies in definition, understanding and implementation. Despite the variability, there seems to be consensus among researchers and practitioners alike on its usefulness in transforming teaching and instructional practices and learning outcomes.

Hord (1997) indicates that professional learning communities (PLCs) engage teachers in a cycle of looking at what is happening in their school, determining if they can make it a better place by changing curriculum, instruction or relationships between community members and assessing the results – all with the goal of enhancing their effectiveness as professionals. A similar point of view is expressed by Stroll et. al. (2006) when they state that PLCs suggest a group of people sharing and critically interrogating their practices in an ongoing, reflective, collaborative, inclusive, learning- oriented, and growth-promoting way. Also, Fulton and Britton (2011) identify the goal of professional learning communities as, "focusing teachers on improving their practice and learning together about how to increase student learning" (p.7). Another group of contributors to the wealth of information present in the literature is DuFour et al. (2008) who define PLCs as educators committed to working collaboratively in ongoing process of collective inquiry and action research to achieve better results for the students they serve. The similarities in the points of view indicate that PLC is not an event, but a process. It involves learners using research to inform and modify curriculum, instruction and assessment tools and strategies. Evident also is collaboration aimed at improvement in teaching practices and learning outcomes.

There are significant benefits to be accrued in a school environment where there is focused intentionality on leadership and collaboration on continuous improvement of learning for all students. Principals recognize that teachers have expertise, can determine their learning needs and that of their colleagues and contribute to student achievement. Teachers can provide leadership to school initiative including professional development. Putnam and Borko (2000) in exploring theories of cognition, declare that thinking and reasoning are most effective when distributed across a system or group, rather than confined to an individual. This concept points to the importance teachers sharing not only their knowledge and expertise on instruction, but also pertinent and relevant information about student learners and strategizing to undertake shared responsibility for enhanced academic achievement. In this environment, individuals can reflect on their instructional practices, share perspectives and collaborate on problem solving, especially on strategies to support underachieving learners. This collaborative approach expands beyond individual classroom and has greater propensity to meet the learning needs of the individual student as he or she journeys from classroom to classroom, grade level to grade level and from school to school. This framework not only has potential to develop teacher expertise, but autonomy, moral purpose and charges within the environment. In this environment, individuals willingly undertake challenges that address the learning gaps identified among the learners from economically deprived communities. Individuals also make cooperate decisions on strategies to effect changes in their learning, collect and carefully analyse evidences on the impact of the strategies employ, modify and or continue their intense collective efforts regardless of outcome and adhere to an agreement to strive for effective teaching and successful learning outcomes. DuFour and Marzano (2011) say, "The focus (of PLCs) must shift from helping individuals become more effective in their isolated classrooms and schools, to creating a new collaborative culture based on interdependence, shared responsibility and mutual accountability" (p.67). Rosenholtz (1991) also feels that teachers' sense of optimism, hope and commitment reside in workplace conditions that enable them to feel professionally empowered and fulfilled.

While a lot can be said for teacher benefits, at the core of a professional learning community is student enhanced academic achievement. Louis and Marks (1998) analyzed data from eight elementary, eight middle and eight high schools to examine the relationship between the quality of professional development community and student achievement and found moderate correlations between the quality of professional collaboration and the classroom pedagogy. They concluded that achievement levels were significantly higher to the extent that the schools were strong professional communities. The moderate correlation established through their data analysis, provides no indication of the frequency, focus, approach or even application of the professional development community. As well, there is no indication of specific assessment data and demographic characteristics of the students in the sample schools that were analyzed prior to the staff development. There may have been intervening variables. However, in spite of the unknown, the possibility that professional development community involvement has impact can be deduced from the findings. Therefore, investigating the strategy using other samples in different situations is worth undertaking.

Vescio, Ross and Adams (2008) articulate the positive effects of professional learning community on teacher performance and student achievement:

> Participation in learning communities' impacts teaching practice as teachers become more student-centred. In addition, teaching culture is improved because the

learning communities increase collaboration, focus on student learning, teacher authority or empowerment, and continuous learning; when teachers participate in a learning community, students benefit as well, as indicated by improved achievement scores overtime (p.88).

This framework for PLCs embodies some of Kanold's (2011) thoughts on features of professional learning communities classified as: excellence in curriculum, instruction and assessment. Educators should ensure the curriculum, instruction and assessments represent the best practices in our profession. While accommodating individual student differences, interests and abilities, excellence demands that educators develop a common, coherent rigorous curriculum that actively engages all students; equity and access for all students. Educators should therefore challenge each student to give his or her best effort intellectually and ethically. Adults must exhibit genuine care and concern for each student and must collectively commit to providing opportunities for students to fully access the curriculum at its rigorous levels; educating as a professional learning community. Leaders and teachers should commit to ongoing professional development as a model of life-long learning. The board, administration, and staff must function in high performing, collaborative, teams focused on student achievement. Staff development is a job-embedded and collaborative process, not a singular event (p.18).

The evidence from the literature review therefore, points to the professional learning community as an opportunity to focus on student achievement using the vehicles of curriculum, assessment and instruction, the development of teacher competence and expertise through collaborative professional development and finally, the development and expansion of sustainable shared leadership capacity. The efforts expended in this approach, has potential to transform classrooms, schools and systems into learning environments that benefit all students. The framework however, hinges on the belief that all students can learn and there is evident, a practice that explicitly demonstrates high expectations for all learners regardless of socioeconomic variables that may challenge their level of achievement. As a result, the mandate must focus building capacity on instructional practices that includes teacher competencies and motivation for all teachers, not just some teachers.

Fullan (2010a) says, "Essentially, capacity building implies that people take the opportunity to do things differently, to learn new skills and to generate more effective practice" (p.57). Sharrat and Fullan (2009) also purport that capacity building must be systemic if it is going to make a performance difference for all students. They argue that capacity building is a highly complex, dynamic, knowledge-building process intended to lead to increased student achievement in every school (p. 8). The evidence is clear that the core purpose of capacity building is enhanced student achievement and the approach involves teacher collaboration and support for each member of the team. Harris and Jones (2010) say that real improvement through professional learning communities (PLCs) focuses on the needs of the learners first and working relentlessly to improve pedagogy so that the learners' needs are effectively met. It can be deduced from the data obtained from principals' interview responses and the literature review that professional learning communities (PLCs) are among the strategies needed to build teaching capacity.

This approach facilitates leadership development, sharing of successful practices, building of supportive systems and a focus on solving challenging problems together. If all teachers share and implement best practices in all of our classrooms, all students should benefit from high quality learning and improve their academic success. This may generate a feeling of fantasy and not reality but is worth expecting and striving to accomplish. The principal respondents in this research identified professional learning communities (PLCs) as a teaching-learning initiative aimed at supporting students living in poverty. Some of the principals offered the following quotations: Principal H says "PLCs are scheduled and led by teachers. Teachers are empowered to take the lead. Teachers work with admin to plan PLCs and Lead teachers met with principal and vice principal on a weekly basis to monitor the PLC implementation and plan the next steps". Principal X comments, "When teachers possess growth mindsets and have high expectations for students they expend efforts and provide opportunities for the students to succeed". Principal N says, "Teacher led PLCs contribute to collaboration and teaching improvement".

The challenge is how to initiate a successful professional learning community. Despite the perceived benefits from the literature review and from the respondents, from my experience, some teachers perceive PLCs as disconnected from the reality of the issues faced in their classes and address too many theories on instructional practices and not many practical strategies. They feel that the opportunities are sometimes planned with little or no teacher input. Some teachers strongly feel they are almost at the end of their careers and what they have being doing has been successful. They do not need to change now. It is also perceived that the opportunities are created from a deficit mindset. This perspective implies teachers need to be fixed. Consequently, they see the sessions as dysfunctional and prefer to spend their time teaching their students. A number of teachers in the sample opined that professional development should be focused on the specific needs of their students, should be opportunities for teachers to work together in teams to improve teaching and student learning and that the primary outcome of the opportunities should be to cultivate in-school expertise in instruction, curriculum and assessment. Some teachers in the sample schools responded consistently with strongly agree or agree to the following items on the questionnaire: Teachers professional learning goals identify the knowledge, skills, practices and dispositions to increase teaching quality and student learning. Teachers focus their professional development on the learning needs of their students. At this school, our professional development opportunities include specific research-based strategies to facilitate learning for students living in poverty. We identify the focus of our professional development by analyzing a variety of student achievement data. Some teachers in the same schools responded consistently to the same items with strongly disagree or disagree. Although perceptions of the same activities can differ significantly, it can also imply that the needs for these activities are different. Consequently, some teachers may perceive benefits from participating in PLCs while others view them as a waste of time. While there cannot be any prescription, as each school situation is unique and one size does not fit all, a model can be developed from the research studies done on the subject. DuFour, DuFour, Eaker and Karhanek (2010) offer the following suggestions and preliminary steps: build share knowledge among teachers and staff regarding the elements of the PLC process and the rationale for implementing these elements; develop the leadership capacity of key teachers to ensure they play a significant role the implementation of the PLC process; assign teachers to meaningful teams whose members work interdependently to achieve common goals for which they accept mutual responsibility; ensure the members of each team are clear on the knowledge, skills and dispositions each student is to acquire as a result of their course or grade level; establish common pacing to monitor student proficiency of the same knowledge and skills and develop a series of district-level and building-level common assessments to monitor the learning of each student (pp. 132-133). Shared knowledge and leadership are key components of any school success. Principals in the sample attributed their schools success to teachers working together in co-planning, co-teaching and using data to monitor students' progress. The principals also believed that shared leadership encourages wider participation and greater efforts in serving their students. If the knowledge and leadership are made to permeate the school and sustained, all the educators will understand what is important and valued and work to accomplish it. Educators also tend to hold one another accountable for the results. If enhanced achievement for students from economically disadvantaged backgrounds is perceived important, all the educators may collaborate to achieve this goal.

The highlighted facets speak to values of clarity, shared knowledge of process, leadership development, meaningful assignment, collaboration, accountability, a focus on data to inform practice and monitoring of student learning. A slight deviation from the steps outlined, maybe to allow teachers the opportunity to choose their own PLC groups based on their own learning needs. Teachers' choices will motivate them to develop a sense of responsibility, secure accountability and produce satisfaction and enhanced performance. However, the success of any approach is heavily dependent on the leadership of the administration.

The individual or individuals must create the environment of trust, collaboration and real involvement. Both administrators and teachers have to sense the need and commitment to improve student learning, recognize their learning needs and be willing to be learners together. Some teachers in this sample in underscoring the impact of principal leadership and teacher collaboration on student academic achievement make these comments, "Principals and teachers work closely together to implement collaborative professional learning teams. Principals and staff share knowledge, research and best practices about professional learning throughout the school. Our principal develops teacher leaders' skills and knowledge in planning and designing school-based professional development". Professional learning communities (PLCs) that include these considerations will improve teaching and learning.

Developing and Sustaining Effective Professional Learning Communities (PLCs)

In my roles as principal and superintendent of education, I have had unique and distinct opportunities to develop, implement and also to observe many different iterations of professional learning communities (PLCs). While there have been variations of processes, action plans, implementation strategies and even challenges across the spectrum, the benefits of developing teacher instructional practices to enhance student academic achievement out-weighs any challenges experienced. Approximately 55% of the teaching staff in the sample believed the professional learning communities impact on student academic achievement. Forty-five percent (45%) of the respondents did not consider PLCs as a contributing factor to students' academic achievement. These individuals could have considered themselves equipped with a plethora of strategies or maybe at the peak of their careers and possess a wealth of expertise. They may even see new directions or changes as events that will pass with time as a result require no need to change practices. Some may even link student achievement to other variables that PLCs cannot address. However, if a half of the teachers felt that PLCs have impact on achievement, it is worth implementing. It may just mean that the other teachers need to be persuaded on the relevance and importance of "all hands on deck" Also, from the quantitative collected and analyzed (at 0.01 level of significance) instruction is correlated with professional learning community (variance 0.910). This significant correlation implies that if teachers are engaged in PLCs there is possibility that achievement will improve. It also implies that lack of participation in PLCs may limit the level of achievement students experience in a particular school. Principals in explaining the factors that contributed to their schools' success identified PLCs as opportunities for teachers to share their skills. One principal said, "I cannot over-emphasize the importance of professional learning communities supported by our learning coaches". The effectiveness of any PLC therefore, rests on the framework embraced, strategies employed in its development and implementation as well as its sustainability. Principals and teachers sometimes move from school to school. However, students sometime remain the most constant population of our schools. Improving their learning is our number one priority. This very important mandate should be the collaborative, relentless and persistent efforts of all staff. To be impactful requires both principals and teachers to assiduously pursue opportunities to develop their expertise.

Eaker, DuFour and DuFour (2002) believe that the framework of professional learning community can be categorized into three themes: the school has to have a solid, shared mission, vision, values and goals; collaborative teams that work interdependently to achieve common goals; and a focus on results as evidenced by a commitment to continuous improvement. The implications, here, are that all players involved in improving student learning must contribute to, and fully buy into, the school's enhanced learning outcomes action plan. Shared mission--learning for all, shared vision--understanding and commitment to the school's core purpose, shared values-- responsibility and accountability to achieve the vision and shared goals--priorities and the timelines, contribute immensely to the success of any PLCs (p. 47).

DuFour et.al. (2010) have offered the suggestions to building the foundation of a PLC: move quickly to action. This swift movement however, should not diminish the value of adequate and authentic consultation that enlists wide staff input; build shared knowledge when asking people to make decision. The more informed the participants in a decision making process are, the greater the probability that diverse views and divergent thinking will result in the best decision. Also, there is the possibility that conflicts and barriers-- when teachers perceive that their professional goals, knowledge and skills are not identified and incorporated in the opportunities being offered, implementation maybe significantly minimized or even eliminated; use this same foundation to assist in day-to-day decisions; use the foundation to identify practices that should be eliminated. In any environment where many facets of school operations and the fulfilment of stakeholders' expectations compete for school personnel's efforts and attention, shared commitment and goals should help the team establish and maintain priority and focus; translate the vision of the school into teachable points of view; write value statements as behaviour rather than beliefs; focus on yourself rather than others; recognize that the process is nonlinear. It should be cyclical and interactive; it is what you do that matters, not what you call it (pp.51-53).

These foundational principles are key to creating a paradigm shift in the learning culture of the school. Therefore, both principals and teacher leaders should pay keen attention to the challenges and issues that have potential to impact on the successful outcomes of PLCs. DuFour and Fullan (2013) offer the following considerations: establish coherence and clarity regarding purpose and priorities throughout the organization; build shared knowledge about the rationale for change; engage in meaningful two-way dialogue throughout the change process; identify the specific steps that must be taken immediately to make progress toward long-term aspirational goals; create a culture that is simultaneously loose and tight; build collective capacity around the agenda of improving student achievement; demonstrate reciprocal accountability by providing the resources and support to help people succeed at what they are being asked to do; establish ongoing feedback loops that help people assess the impact of their efforts and make adjustments accordingly; ensure transparency of results, and using the results to inform and improve practice; create a collaborative culture in which people take collective responsibility for the success of the initiative; sustain the improvement process and celebrate small wins (p. 19).

Sometimes all of these seemingly grand ideas may seem attractive, but their application could be challenging and overwhelming. One caution is prudent. Individuals should view the suggested ideas as just suggestions, make decisions on those to be explored and experimented with as well as those ideas that can be melded with existing initiatives. For example, developing a collaborative culture, collective responsibility, self-efficacy and a sustainable improvement process should be features on any effective PLCs. These features should allow PLCs to outlast changes in administration and staff. When a particular principal is transferred as practised in our schools, the culture of learning established, knowledge and expertise developed and made to permeate the school stand a good chance of continuing. The strength and effectiveness of the practices may even attract the attention and participation of the new administrator. This continuation of effective practice may prevent the skewing of student academic achievement because of changes in leadership, teaching staff or even student cohorts. In responding to the interview question that asked principals to identify other factors that contributed to their schools' success, some responses provided were: stability in administration, effective succession plan and high teacher retention rate. Principals say, "When principals remain in the same school for a number of years, they can initiate changes and see them materialize. The teachers stay here because they want to make a difference. Whenever principals have to change schools, the successors should have demonstrated expertise in serving similar community of learners and families." This implies that frequent movement of leadership is not encouraged, but where the need necessitates movement or change, there should be a carefully thought-out succession plan is recommended.

Once there is shared knowledge and understanding of certain beliefs and procedural strategies, the leaders must attend to organizing the various teams. The literature contains many pertinent examples of valuable advice on appropriate next steps and strategies to monitor and evaluate PLC actions. These include: all core subject, or division teachers are organized in small relevant groups; all collaborative groups receive collaborative time per week requiring mandatory attendance; teachers in these groups, examine achievement data on their own students and use the data to inform, adjust and improve their instruction and accelerate student learning; school administrative teams and data coaches meet monthly to discuss the status of the work and administrators take steps to remediate a teacher or teachers who did not participate in the collaborative team or were disruptive to the team process. (Delaware Department of Education, 2010, p. C27, cited in cited in DuFour and Fullan, 2013, p. 8)

Principal H says, "Good assessment data are used to inform differentiated instruction. We spend a lot of time in our PLCs studying data and developing action plans to make necessary changes". Principal G says, "Data allows us to assess learning needs, determine student progress and remediation strategies". Principal D says, "Teachers feel supported by administrators. Teachers at this school share their skills." It is very likely that a practice of sharing expertise developed over time will become the norm and outlast changes in administration. As a result of the literature review, my practice and experience, I offer the following suggestions to schools in their efforts to develop a sustainable PLC model. At initial stage do a need assessment. Collect and analyse multiple sources of (qualitative, quantitative and perceptual) data in order to identify students' learning needs, teacher expertise, motivation, commitment, systems, practices and procedures already existing and changes needed. Develop shared mission, vision, values and goals. Use the SMART (specific, measurable, achievable, relevant and timely) goal development strategy to establish purpose, priorities and actions. Develop an action plan and enlist further input for clarification and greater support. Follow the action plan, but create room for flexibility and modification. As the leader, show genuine interest in working towards a successful outcome. As well, empower and develop shared leadership and accountability for achievement of the established goals. Collect and analyse data through classroom visits (purposeful and transparent), walkthroughs - use non- evaluative questions to discuss and reflect on observations. Focus attention on observed student learning, thinking or gaps. Use information to inform pedagogy. Create opportunities to share and celebrate successes without creating unhealthy rivalry or competition. Create a shared culture of teacher leadership, collaboration, trusting relationships, commitment to student achievement that is systemic, focused, intentional and lasting. This PLC sustainability should out-last changes in school personnel. (Adopted from DuFour et. al., 2010)

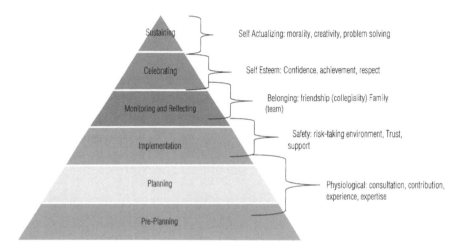

Figure 4.1 A Model For Developing Sustainable PLC

Figure 4.1 is an adaption of Maslow's hierarchy of needs pyramid. This pictorial representation capitalizes on the theory of human motivation-actions directed toward goal attainment as an approach to achieve sustainable PLCs (Maslow, 1943). The diagram portrays both the physiological (lower level) needs and the psychological (upper level) needs. At the lower level, the staffs' physiological needs are met at the pre-planning and planning stages. Here, staff are consulted, their experience, expertise and contributions identified and incorporated in the school's PLC action plan. Their psychological needs do not surface until these basic needs are met. Staffs who have come to these stages of the process at a higher needs level, will probably embrace the initiative immediately. However, time and effort should be invested in laying the ground work to achieve whole staff commitment in implementation. Any PLC plan developed without carefully addressing these needs run the risk of limiting successful outcomes.

At the implementing stage, there are the safety needs: risk taking, trusting relationships and need for support. Here, the staffs need to feel that they operate in an environment to creatively problem solve, think outside the box and be supported rather than evaluated; they can be honest about their level of knowledge and expertise or lack thereof, and receive advice and guidance. They feel free to have open and honest discussions and experience the trust of their colleagues to assist them in the achievement of the corporate goals.

The monitoring and reflecting stage offers opportunities to demonstrate a sense of belonging. Individuals solidify their idea of team through collegiality and friendship. The celebrating stage is likened to Maslow's self-esteem stage. Staffs now reflect on their journey of planning and implementing together, their accomplishments, gain even greater respect from colleagues for significant contributions to the team's success, develop confidence to undertake even greater challenges and further explore new ideas. These attributes build self-esteem. An accomplished and confident staff will experience job satisfaction and demonstrate high morale. These are necessary ingredients for an effective and sustainable PLC.

Lastly, the sustaining stage is the self-actualizing stage. Staffs now have developed morality, creativity and collective problem-solving expertise. At this stage, their actions are motivated by their desire for personal growth. They also possess the propensity to further their own continuous growth and to influence the growth of their colleagues. This level of organizational development has potential for capacity building among practitioners and has potential to transform a school into a learning environment for all. It is very likely that this level of self-actualization and the motivation to grow will become permanent, contagious and unstoppable. Principal and teacher turn-over should have little or no negative effect on this kind of movement.

Principals when asked to explain the high level of student success at their schools, some responded, "Teacher efficacy and collaboration are key to student success. Teachers don`t give on students and don't subscribe to deficit model. Teachers have growth mindset and have high expectations for all students. Every student writes EQAO tests and there is no exemption". Principals believe in their teachers and the teachers believe in themselves and their students. Teachers also believe that their collective efforts can make a difference in enhancing student success. PLCs therefore, should become a significant function of any school's operation.

Crucial to the effectiveness and sustainability of any PLC is the attention paid to developing the school as a learning organization (Senge,1992). Through PLCs, principals and teachers are afforded the opportunities to address their learning needs while focusing on the learning needs of their students. Traditionally, professional learning communities and professional development were viewed as distractions from the work, but the new paradigm views these opportunities as the "work". Collaborating and sharing responsibilities for students' learning and managing behavioural challenges become the work of the team rather than that of just an individual. The greater the collective level of expertise, the less onerous the task and more manageable the work. Therefore a focus on adult learning opportunities should include job embedded learning focusing on developing the collective and not just the individual. PLCs should be aligned with school goals in order to establish relevance and to ensure continuity. PLCs should also be linked specifically to enhanced student academic achievement and provide individual the opportunities to evaluate the success of the opportunities based on data showing higher levels of student success.

While the principles, recommended strategies and suggestions should not be viewed as a panacea, their careful consideration and skilful application as deemed necessary, should produce recognizable and positive learning outcomes for all participants. This should bring schools closer to fulfilling their mandate-- higher level of student achievement for all learners.

Teachers' Professional Learning Community Mindset

Throughout my entire educational career serving in many local and international jurisdictions in leading and supervisory roles, I have encountered and learned from phenomenal, transformative, competent, innovative, creative and extremely skilful practitioners. These teacher leaders have worked conscientiously, scrupulously and relentlessly in changing learning outcomes for individuals especially those from very disadvantaged backgrounds. Conversely, there have been practitioners whose knowledge and skills could be greatly enhanced. However, the total success of any educational system rests on the continuous, purposeful and intentional development of its administrators and other leaders.

Today, as never before, there is a heightened expectation that our schools improve academic achievement for all students. Our classrooms are populated with students from very diverse backgrounds, demographics, ethnicities, socioeconomic statuses, geographies, languages, and levels of prior learning to name a few. The complexities and challenges presented by this diversity, comprises the greatest strength—a richness of resources to be proud of in any learning environment. This richness requires our schools to embrace learning for all as a focused way of conducting their core business. In this "learning for all" environment, there is a belief that all students can learn, principals and teachers subscribe to the fact that they can make a difference and are constantly engaged in opportunities to improve their practice- fine-tune their craft. There needs to be a shared belief in the collaborative development of expertise rather than just the expertise of single individuals. In a transformative learning environment, the emphasis is developing competence in all. All classrooms should buzz with instructional strategies that address diverse learning needs, strive for enhanced achievement, but also possess practitioners who believe and share challenges, practices and learning from research aimed at positively impacting student learning outcomes. McCann et. al. (2012) say, "If schools are going to experience genuine reform and significant improvement, the administrators and other leaders in the schools will have to focus on improving the quality of teaching, no matter how good they think the teaching is at the moment" (p.149) Therefore, to achieve learning for all requires a shift in belief, assumptions, attitudes and focus (Eaker and Keating, 2015). They state that focus on learning, teacher expectations, Self-efficacy, reflections on how students learn best and continuous professional development are attributes crucial to the effectiveness of any PLC.

These attributes have potential to either negatively or positively impact on assessment, instruction and learning. DuFour (2007) posits that student learning depends on every teacher learning all the time. Also, in his differentiation between instructional leadership and "learning leader" points out that the latter is focused on whether learning is taking place; there is monitoring of the instructional practices with a special emphasis on the outcome of the instruction. In a school with teachers collectively and intentionally demonstrating these attributes positively, the emphasis is not on the perceived gaps in talents from students of lower socioeconomic backgrounds, but an emphasis on strategies and innovative instructional practices that capitalize on the strengths of each learner, creating opportunities and providing supports for each student to be purposefully engaged and flourish academically.

Ronald Edmonds (1979) in exploring, "Effective schools for the Urban Poor", concludes that high performing schools embrace accountability for learning. They believe that lack of academic experience and or home support may slow down the learning process for selected students, but they do not allow it to control their beliefs about these students' ability to learn; they expect and demand high performance and do not use students' backgrounds as excuse for low expectations. In these schools, teachers take full responsibility for student academic achievement and hold the assumption that all students are capable of acquiring specific knowledge and developing high level of academic skills. This assumption is commensurate with Carol Dweck's (2006) growth mindset proponent: that ability is changeable and can be developed through learning. In an atmosphere where this is the pervasive assumption and belief, where instructional practices mirror the belief and learners are offered the opportunities to excel, students from even disadvantage socioeconomic backgrounds rise to the challenge and even some time, out-perform their counter-parts from very affluent backgrounds.

Since the literature clearly establishes the link between teachers' mindset or belief and its impact on student achievement, it is pertinent to explore how a change in belief or mindset can transform learning environments and outcomes.

Dweck (2006), from her research, identified two sets of beliefs that people have about students' intelligence. She describes these as fixed mindset that believes that intelligence is static and some students are smart and some are not. On the other hand, she describes what she believes is a growth mindset. This mindset embraces the belief that intelligence can be developed by various means. One of the media through which schools attempt to develop intelligence is through instructional practices. While the leadership of the administration is instrumental in this effort, the chief architect of intelligence development in the classroom environment is the teacher leader. Rheinberg (cited in Dweck, 2006) conducted a study on the impact of teacher mindset on student achievement. He found that when teachers had a fixed mindset, the students who entered their class as low achievers left as low achievers at the end of the year. Conversely, when teachers had a growth mindset, many of the students who started the year as low achievers progressed to moderate or high achievers. In classrooms, teachers demonstrate their belief by exploring and using instructional practices that make a difference. In these contexts, teachers perceive their roles to be much more than just teaching curriculum, but also teaching students. They recognize that students come to the learning environment and learning tasks with varying levels of readiness. Consequently, through effective assessment practices that make use of a variety of assessment tools, teachers identify knowledge skills and understanding each student demonstrates. This assessment data is then used to inform teaching and learning. The data facilitates the selection of learning activities, pedagogy and monitoring strategies. Also, this paradigm change in curricular delivery approach, encourages teacher-student collaboration in setting learning expectations, strategies to meeting these expectations, supports available and specifically how the expectations will be measured. Teachers then create realistic challenges for each learner without lowering expectations. Students find different entry points in each task and achieve different levels of success and move to different mastery level with support. They continue to receive authentic descriptive feedback at each stage, incorporate the feedback into their revision in order to improve the quality of their performance. The key premise is that when teachers perceive students as capable, they provide opportunities and support to help them achieve academically. If this becomes common belief that inform practice in the classroom, a change in the achievement of under achieving school maybe highly probable. Good, Rattan and Dweck (2007) in studying "teacher effects in mindset intervention outcomes" found that teachers who have been influenced to believe in a growth mindset in mathematics encouraged students who had failed to work harder and further more recommended specific learning strategies that would help them improve, Conversely, teachers who had been influenced to believe in a fixed mindset, tended to comfort students who had failed by telling them that some students are good in mathematics and others are not. This behaviour not only reinforces fixed mindset, but perpetuates negative stereotypes. On the other hand, the growth mindset approach, although specifically referred to mathematics, may be even applicable to other subject areas. Stipek (1996) opines that teachers exert influence on student motivation and achievement through the instructional practices they use, the feedback they give students and other day-to-day interactions with students. Principal interviewees say, "We connect students' histories and experiences to the curriculum. Teachers plan instructions using social justice lens-- justice experienced based on distribution of wealth, opportunities and privileges in society. We study various data and use the information to determine who is achieving and who is not. This information then informs our instructional strategies and remediation."

The literature also highlights some benefits of growth mindset as well as associated instructional practices that impact on student achievement. There is the feeling that growth mindset training can increase test scores. Growth mindset training can increase test scores;

growth mindedness causes students to use deeper learning strategies and to better recover from an initial poor grade; and teaching with a growth mindset seems to decrease or even close achievement gap (Blackwell, et. at., 2007; Grant and Dweck, 2003). Principals in this sample say, "At our PLCs, we focus on growth mindset and barriers to student achievement. We connect students' histories and experiences to the curriculum. Teachers plan instructions using social justice lens-- recognition that access to opportunities is linked to wealth, power and privileges." Teaching students to recognize the influences of these powerful forces, but not allowing them to limit or hinder their achievement is an outstanding teaching learning strategy.

There are also some associated instructional practices associated with benefits which include: establishing high expectations and challenge students to know that they have the ability to meet these expectations, creating risk-tolerant learning environment that values challenge-seeking, learning and efforts above perfection, giving feedback focused on progress, not ability or intelligence and reinforce the idea that our brains develop through effort and learning (Blackwell, Trezesniewski and Dweck, 2007).

These benefits and practices should not be viewed on their individual merit and not be seen as a panacea, but as considerations necessary to encourage and facilitate enhanced academic achievement for all learners. They could also serve to motivate the exploration of creative strategies of equal pedagogical value. Both Gore, Griffiths and Ladwig (2004) and Lingard, Hayes and Mills (2003) subscribe to the idea that classrooms filled with dialogue, inquiry, collaboration, innovation, connectivity and creative practices are the hallmarks of effective contemporary pedagogy. This point of view speaks to and supports the stance that the collaborative efforts of classroom teachers impact student learning. This current researcher recognizes and ascribes to the idea that "total expertise" resides in the collective rather than in the individual. Principals have expertise and teachers have expertise. These individuals who hold these respective positions should not function in silos. They should share their expertise and resources in an attempt to better serve all of their students. Consequently, the more collaboration a school experiences in shared leadership and instructional practices, the greater the possibility of improving academic achievement. O'Brien (2012) feels that teachers need to see the qualities of their students and their personal teaching capabilities through a flexible, fluid lens in order to effectively facilitate creative pedagogical experiences.

Stein (2014) opines that when teachers nurture a growth mindset, students focus on the efforts they put into a task rather than falling back on pre-conceived beliefs about their intelligence or skills. Learning happens when they push through their comfort zones. Classrooms should therefore, become learning environments where students naturally apply efforts and persistence to achieve. In the same vein, teachers should not focus on preconceived beliefs of students' gaps in learning, stereotypes based on demographic data such as SES, but rather on the instructional strategies necessary to facilitate learning. There should be openness in recognizing their current level of expertise and a willingness to capitalize on opportunities to build teaching-learning capacity. Stein offers the following strategies to build this capacity: embrace your personal-mindset journey; teachers should get in touch with their own personal mindset stories, experiences that connect them to who they are and form the basis of their thinking and beliefs of how people learn, embrace the experiences and adjust lessons to empower students; collaborate personally and professionally; make time to check in with self daily, journal thoughts and key ideas that express feelings, keep emotions in check and in sharing ideas with others; know your students by connecting with them beyond content; create a community of learners by being involved in a professional learning community, create and participate in professional development opportunities; keep academic content accessible to all learners and find the balance between what is taught and how it is taught. Instil in students, a focus on the process of learning (Education Week, 2014, p.3).

The evidence from the literature review, points to the fact that teachers need to develop and demonstrate a growth mindset, inculcate the same in their students and creatively allow this belief to permeate the learning environment in order to improve achievement for all learners. The evidence from the principals' data in this study also links professional learning communities (PLCs) to improved student academic achievement. All the schools in the sample have been engaged in PLCs. Despite their challenges, their student achievement has exceeded Ministry, Board and even school and community expectations. These schools have even outperformed some schools serving more affluent students. Attempts then should be made to explore and implement PLCs as a viable strategy to improve academic achievement especially for student from economically disadvantaged backgrounds.

The classroom teachers are still the single most significant contributors to student achievement; the effect of their contribution is greater than that of parents, peers, the entire school or poverty (Hanushek, 2005; Rockoff, 2004). Teachers have to believe that every student can achieve regardless of their SES, Special Education needs, race, achievement gaps or any perceived challenged they exhibit. Coupled with this belief, teachers must feel that they have the expertise necessary to move the achievement of all their students to a higher level. They must be willing to provide all their students access to high quality instruction and learning activities that motivate them to produce excellent outcomes-- above expectations.

No one teacher can achieve this result regardless of the expertise possessed, but collectively groups of teachers can accomplish greater results. All that a student learns is not learned in one classroom with one teacher. Students continue to build on their learning from one grade level to the other, from one classroom to the other and from one school to the other. Therefore, it is pertinent that good quality instruction permeates all classrooms and schools. As the learning needs students bring to the learning environment become more complex, teachers must continue to develop their expertise. They must continue to learn and grow together and share the expertise developed from research and experience. PLCs should be implemented as opportunities that help teachers achieve their aspiration to equip themselves to be outstanding practitioners, fully self-actualized knowing that they have contributed significantly to the enhanced academic achievement of all their students.

CHAPTER FIVE

PROFESSIONAL DEVELOPMENT

Teachers undertake their responsibility of successfully providing equitable learning opportunities for students to maximize their learning with varying degrees of training, expertise and even a repertoire of skills. The expertise developed maybe be shaped by personal experiences and both formal and informal professional development. However, the expertise possessed must be applied in an environment with diverse learners and sometimes constant educational policy directional changes. The challenge seems to intensify when the educator gets a job in an inner-city school populated with students from economically disadvantaged communities. The reality of this job opportunity may require teachers to reflect on their training and take the necessary steps to fine tune their skills in order to demonstrate effective practice. According to Guskey (2000), "Never before in this history of education has greater importance been attached to the professional development of teachers. Every proposal for educational reform and every plan for school improvement, emphasizes the need for high-quality professional development" (p. 3). This statement is even more relevant today and the need more urgent. The Ontario Ministry of Education issued, "Education That Works For You" (2019) mandated a four year mathematics strategy to ensure students have a strong understanding of math fundamentals and how to apply them, Science, Technology,

Engineering and Math (STEM) strategies, E-learning, Financial Literacy, Indigenous Education and Digital Curriculum. Included in the package is mandatory additional math qualification requirement for teachers. Another reality is that the rate of poverty increases in the city (Toronto Child and Family Poverty Report: Municipal Election Edition, 2018). Ten wards in the city have child poverty rate between 33% and 47%. Even wards with relatively low poverty rates have double or triple the ward average. The reality is, there are pockets of poverty across the entire city. Students' lived experiences should inform the teaching strategies aimed at enhancing their academic achievement consequently, their life chances.

Another factor for careful consideration is teachers who received their formal professional training in other jurisdictions, evaluated and now certified by the Ontario College of Teachers to practise in Ontario classrooms. These educators need to be familiar with policies, practices, learners and learning environments among other variables that can impact on their students' learning. As a new comer to the Canadian teaching profession, I had to learn new things quickly. I took many additional qualification courses, but also filled my learning gap through informal learning: book club, mentorship opportunities, and participation in workshops, seminars and conferences. I continue to embrace the concept of education as a continuous process and cherish the idea that my learning is linked to my students' achievement. I therefore perceive professional development as my continuous learning to improve the way I teach. Each school year, my assigned students and their profiles change; there are new teaching strategies to be explored and experimented with, new ministry directives and other environmental changes to be considered in order to maximize my teaching effectiveness. I continue to pursue graduate studies and share my learning and resources with colleagues. From the quantitative data collected, 57% of the teachers perceived that professional development contributed to student academic achievement. Also, principals in responding to the question on the strategies used to engage staff understanding the attributes and functions necessary to help students living in poverty, unanimously identified professional development.

According to the respondents, professional development provides teachers the opportunities to work collaboratively, share resources, expertise and celebrate success stories with one another. Teachers study various data, identify underachievers, share best practices, plan instructions using social justice lens and connect students' histories and experiences to the curriculum. Although there was no commonality established in frequency and approaches, it was evident that the focus at each school was on student achievement.

The literature contains various insights and views on teachers' professional development. There is a range of views on rationale, designs, strategies, effectiveness or ineffectiveness. One school of thought embraces a deficit mindset with a belief that teachers lack professional competence and need training (Imants and van Veen, 2010). Teachers however, undertake their responsibilities with varying degrees of formal training and expertise. Their qualifications sometimes include degrees, diplomas, certificates at the under-graduate and graduate levels. They possess a wealth of content knowledge and pedagogical expertise. They may just need some professional support and guidance in the application of the knowledge and expertise. Different aspects of their work, changes in student demographics, curriculum expectations, assessment and evaluation practices may require professional development.

The other school of thought recognizes that the most significant contributor to student achievement is the teacher. Hattie (2012) says, "Expert teachers have high level of knowledge and deep outcomes, can successfully monitor learning and provide feedback that assists students to progress, can attend to the more attitudinal attributes of learning and can provide defensible evidence of positive impacts of teaching on student learning" (p.24). This belief has potential to trigger a design of professional development opportunities which involve principal and teacher collaboration. In a school that is populated with a significant number of students from economically disadvantaged communities, principals and teachers should collect and analyse data from multiple sources to identify students' learning needs, determine instructional strategies to maximize their achievement, identify gaps if any, in teacher competence and commit to work together on developing their expertise consequently, enhancing student achievement. Crandall and Finn-Miller (2014) purport that sustained, content-focused professional development is most effective when it actively involves teachers in concrete ways and is concentrated on specific instructional practices rather than abstract discussions of teaching. This approach allows the team of teachers to develop consensus, take responsibility and accountability for developing and implementing professional development opportunities and together objectively evaluate their outcomes. Also, this approach recognizes that teachers are professionals and should be instrumental in designing their learning opportunities. In doing so, they can reflect on the strategies, their individual and collective learning outcomes and the impact of their learning on their students' achievement. The data collected from their reflection can also be used to evaluate the past opportunities and inform the decisions on future opportunities.

The reports and reviews of the literature on professional development portray consistency in some designs: presentations, workshops, seminars, additional qualification courses, the benefits and effectiveness of the opportunities, but present insufficient data to logically and directly link professional development to student achievement. Although the correlations of the benefits are clearly articulated, the nuances and variety of the approaches-- school directed, teacher initiated and led, consistency in the offerings, location of the opportunities (on-site or off-site), expectations (mandatory or voluntary) present challenges in evaluating the effectiveness and in establishing direct link between the opportunities and student learning. The challenge is compounded when we examine the plethora of variables that impact on student learning such as socioeconomic status, attendance, behaviour, motivation as well as using a single data point such as EQAO to measure the effectiveness of the teacher's instructional strategies. Could the use of measures like these, while they have merits narrow the focus of instruction, minimize the use of effective formative assessment practices and consequently, limit student achievement? Todd (2015) believes that evidence-based teaching consists of evidence of practice, evidence in practice and evidence of practice. Evidence of practice involves teachers' knowledge of effective practice gleaned through reading research studies and articles. The evidence in practice is transferring the lessons learned to the planning and implementation of instruction. Evidence of practice requires the teacher to collect qualitative and quantitative data on students' learning. Here, conducting authentic assessment, providing feedback and using information to inform instruction could lead to enhanced achievement for all learners. Also, professional development could be the vehicle used to disaggregate data, share knowledge of research-based strategies and collaborate on instruction, evaluate implementation and determine next steps.

In conducting this research, principals were asked to identify the strategies they used to help their staff develop understanding of the attributes and functions necessary to help students living in poverty succeed. The responses included: a focus on professional development and instructional practices. They used these opportunities to study various data, determine achievement gaps, address growth mindset, barriers to student achievement, share expertise, resources, success stories, connect students' histories and experiences to the curriculum and collaborate on instruction using social justice lens. When asked how staff developed instructional capacity that included research-based practices to enhance academic achievement for students from poor communities, respondents again identified professional development and highlighted activities such as co-planning, co-teaching, developing common assessment tools and using these instruments to monitor students' progress. Staff meetings were used to engage teachers in conversations on instruction. As well, there were frequent uses of "Learning Buddies" where teachers work in small groups or in pairs to share expertise. Other professional development opportunities referenced were Collaborative Inquiry or Theory of Action----a form of teacher action research. Principals also used "Accountable Talk", an approach that leads teachers to reflect on their practice, identify areas for improvement and strategies to effect the changes. This approach includes follow up and a feedback loop for both administrators and teachers to evaluate the success achieved and mutually agree on further action plan and next steps. Question 5 of the principals' questionnaire asked principals to identify professional development opportunities provided to staff implementing teaching-learning initiatives to support students living in poverty. The respondents identified strategies such as: teacher led professional learning communities, professional dialogues, "teachable moments" and "Instructional Rounds" or "Walkthroughs".

Despite the different views on the elements that contribute to effective teacher professional development, there was an agreement that it positively impacts on student achievement. Easton (2004) opines that professional development helps to deepen educators' content knowledge and ability to provide instruction and assessment so that students can meet high academic standards. Marzano, Walters and McNulty (2005) feel that the most frequently mentioned resources important to effective functioning of a school is professional development opportunities for teachers. From the evidence in the literature and the data collected from principal and teacher respondents, one can conclude that professional development allows teachers to collaborate and share expertise to enhance their competence and student achievement. While this conclusion should hold true for all schools, it is even more important in schools that serve a significant population of students from high poverty backgrounds. These students' lived experiences are varied, challenging and complex. Therefore, continuous teacher professional development maybe the determining factor in raising the achievement level in under-performing schools.

Co-Planning and Co-Teaching

Administrators, teachers and students believe that they can make a difference in student achievement. There seems to be the perception that collaboration enhances learning outcomes. The principals in the sample, when asked to identify other factors that contributed to the success of their schools, identified co-planning and co-teaching as strategies. Their responses characterized the engagement as: "Teachers are most important, but principals make a difference". "At this school, we involve teachers and coaches in planning, classroom instruction and student learning". "Teachers tell us that they appreciate admin support and feel we have their backs." While they believed in collaboration, they also believed both principals and teachers should intensify their efforts to effectively fulfill their roles in student achievement. Teachers, in an attempt to fulfill their mandate, have been using co-planning and co-teaching as strategies to enhance academic achievement for the students they serve. These strategies also serve as professional development opportunities. Teachers collaborate with colleagues and coaches to plan and deliver instructions and to learn from one another. These strategies create the potential for teachers to improve their practice through dialogue on curriculum, teaching and assessment strategies and student learning needs. Principals' responses to the interview question: How do you and your staff develop instructional capacity that includes research-based practices to enhance academic achievement for students from poor communities? (question 4) identified learning together through co-planning and co-teaching as strategies. The principals replied, "We frequently participate in co-planning and co-teaching. Co-planning and co-teaching facilitate the use of data to monitor student progress". Winks (2017) believes that teacher improvement is linked to school improvement and student learning outcomes. He also believes that the goal of creating an excellent teacher for every classroom only becomes a reality when the education profession and its leaders define teacher excellence not as a condition, but as a process of continuous improvement over time. This belief clearly implies the need for educators to continue learn and grow- a recognition that expertise is always developing in a changing environment. Professional development therefore keeps practitioners on the cutting edge of their craft.

Co-planning brings teachers from the same school, other schools and even from the school board together to plan lessons or units. In the planning process, students' learning expectations are identified and clustered around the curricular ideas the teachers plan to deliver. Teachers explore teaching and learning strategies, develop rich tasks and practise the tasks themselves, In this scenario, teachers preempt students challenges, misunderstandings and misconceptions. They also pre-develop rich questions to prompt thinking, expand understanding and to facilitate enhance achievement.

Teachers are not only engaged in the co-planning process, but extend this process to co-teaching. Here, members of the co-planning team engage in teaching the planned lesson or lessons to a group of students. One of the teachers teaches the lesson while another teacher serves as participant observer. The group then reconvenes to deliberate on students' responses on the content, teaching strategies, interactions with the teacher and engagement with their peers. They collect data to support assessment strategies, make decisions about students who have not yet mastered the learning outcomes and plan the next steps including additional opportunities to be provided to underachieving students.

Co-planning and co-teaching allow teachers to develop their expertise, collaborate on instructional practices, focus on student achievement, to enlist support from administrators in terms of common scheduled time for meeting as well as payment for supply teacher coverage. The principals in the sample said they used some inner-city model school funds for this purpose. Teachers draw on the expertise of learning coaches---- a practice in the Toronto District School Board. All these opportunities can support teacher development and can enhance student academic achievement.

Instructional Rounds

Many teachers intentionally and consistently employ teaching practices aimed at improving achievement for the diverse learners in their classrooms. Each year, the group of learners changes and so do the learners' learning needs. This reality requires teachers to explore and use a variety of teaching strategies to enhance students' academic achievement. Consequently, teachers' involvement in different professional development activities becomes not only crucial, but necessary and pertinent. Through professional development opportunities, teachers focus their attention on their instructional practices, efforts to measure the effects of their practices, collaborate on developing new strategies and learn from one another. At the core of improving instructional practices should be observation. Schools have been using many approaches labeled as instructional rounds, walkthroughs, learning walks and classroom visits. While these approaches are intended to improve, support and share instructional strategies, they are sometimes perceived by teachers to be evaluative-- attempts to highlight and document weaknesses for the purposes of dismissal or other forms of retribution. However, instructional rounds can serve as effective professional development strategy if there is agreement on purpose, process and the equitably application of the strategy to all teachers and in all classrooms. With human subjectivity, achieving equitable practice maybe challenging, but instructional improvement is not impossible. The principals in this study when asked how they monitor and measure the effectiveness of the instructional practices developed through the teachers' participation in professional development indentified: use of data (100%), instructional rounds (80%), walkthroughs (60%) and classroom visits (40%). The teachers in the sample of this study, believe that an emphasis on high levels of achievement, students performing authentic and relevant tasks, inquiry-based, experiential, active learning opportunities are strategies that increased teaching quality and student learning outcomes.

The practices, walkthroughs, learning walks, and classroom visits were sometimes referred to as instructional rounds, described similarly and the terms used interchangeably by the principals. Regardless of the label, the practice as described involved teams of teachers, administrators and sometimes coaches who visit classrooms to observe instruction in a focused, systematic, purposeful and collective way (City, Elmore, Fiarman and Teitel, 2011). The teams can be comprised of teachers from the same school and or different schools. Other principals and superintendent(s) may join the teams. However, regardless of the composition of the team, the instructional rounds process includes a number of steps: develop a problem of practice or hypothesis, classroom observation, observation debrief - reflecting on the effective practices observed during the visit and discussion on improving the strategies.

At the beginning stage of the instructional rounds process, the principal and teachers meet, disaggregate data from a variety of sources and ask some questions, for example: "What sub-group of students is underachieving? What are we going to do about it? What strategies will enhance the academic achievement for this group of students? What do teachers need to support the students who are underachieving?" The sub-group of students could be Special Needs Learners, English as a Second Learners or students from economically disadvantaged communities. The problem of practice discussion should lead to a strategy for intervention formulated in a hypothesis for example: "If we use differentiated instructions, academic achievement will improve for students from poor communities". Once the strategy is agreed on and the professional development needs determined, then the team participates in the training and implementation. The teacher respondents to the questionnaire (57%) believed that instructional practices are associated with academic development is associated with academic achievement. Fifty-five percent (55%) of the teachers believed that professional The principals believed that professional development and professional learning communities (PLCs) impacted instructional practices and was associated to the level of success achieved by their schools.

The second phase of the instructional rounds process is the classroom observation. Here, the team of teachers visits classrooms to observe the implementation of the agreed on teaching strategy. However, prior to the visit, discussions on the "look-fors" become crucial. These discussions serve to minimize subjectivity and keep the focus on the instruction. A Reminder to the team that the aim of the practice is learning and not evaluation is prudent. During the observation, teachers unobtrusively take notes on what teachers do and how students respond.

The next step of the process is debriefing. Teachers meet to discuss their observations. A caution at this stage is to keep the comments specific to what is observed and exclude editorials. Managing effectively this part of the process is crucial to its success. The team constantly needs to be reminded that the participants are taking risks at making themselves vulnerable by opening their classrooms and practices for scrutiny. Teachers need to trust the integrity of the process, confidentiality in the collection and use of the data, fairness of the process and benefits to be achieved. These are ingredients necessary for continuation and sustainability of this practice.

The final stage of the process after analyzing the data collected from the observation is decision on the next steps: need more time for practice and observation, need to fine tune strategy, more professional development among others.

Instructional rounds as a professional development opportunity can only be successful if it is clearly understood by the participants and effectively implemented. The success is dependent on persuasive and supportive leadership. Although the strategy has potential to improve achievement as concluded by principals and teachers, it should be noted that they employed other strategies. Teitel (2009) says, "Although the rounds process is not a silver bullet that will single-handedly lead to better test scores or increase learning for students, it is a powerful accelerant of school and district improvement efforts" (p. 3). Instructional rounds links students' learning needs directly to specific instructional practices and has the potential to make teachers' professional development intentional, relevant and focused. Teachers have opportunities to collaborate and develop their expertise. Students' academic achievement is then enhanced.

CHAPTER SIX

INSTRUCTIONAL PRACTICE

Schools and more specifically teachers have been mandated the responsibility for higher levels of student achievement. The complexities and nuances involved in defining the scope and expected outcome of the mandate create opportunities for constant exploration of different strategies by all those who are engaged in educating students. Students have diverse learning needs, come from diverse backgrounds, have diverse lived experiences, interests and come from diverse communities. This diversity speaks to the unique identities and needs of the individual student, but also the similarities, shared experiences and values each brings to the learning environment. Students from economically disadvantaged backgrounds bring rich diversity to the classroom and should be part of what Tomlinson (2014) describes as "learning profile". Students' learning profiles are determined by their intelligence preferences (verbal-linguistic, logical-mathematical, visual-spatial, bodily-kinesthetic, interpersonal, intrapersonal and existentialist), gender, cultures and or learning styles. These unique identities can shape how they learn and should inform the instructional practices aimed at maximizing their learning outcomes. Students may prefer to learn alone or in small groups, some may learn from the macro to the micro approach where the overall encompassing big ideas are presented and linked to smaller specific parts; some students may prefer the use of concrete examples while others prefer logical or analytical approaches; some thrive on the creative application of the concepts learned (Tomlinson, 2014, p. 19).

The challenge each teacher faces is to understand students' similarities and differences and incorporate this knowledge in the shaping of the instructional practices. According to Earl (2003) differentiation of the instruction is ensuring that each student gets the right learning task at the right time. She further purports that once each student's learning needs are identified, differentiation is not an option. Karten (2015) says, "Differentiation of the instruction (DI) approaches consider student achievement levels, prior knowledge, interests and strengths to vary the content, process and product during the planning, instruction and assessment stages. DI includes appropriate and meaningful tasks, flexible groupings and tiered instruction. This approach is interrelated with students' multiple intelligences, universal designs, interests levels and learning profiles to offer both communications and challenges to the diverse learners who are present in the inclusive classrooms" (p.108).

The strategy, differentiated instruction (DI) seems connected to teachers' knowledge and understanding of each learner and the use of diverse instructional approaches to teach and provide multiple ways and opportunities for each learner to demonstrate expected learning outcomes. Differentiated Instruction therefore connects opportunities to demonstrate learning to students' learning profiles. The implication is that teachers should possess both content and pedagogical knowledge. Gess-Newsome (2013) says, "A unique knowledge base held by teachers that allows them to consider the structure and importance of an instructional topic, recognize the features that will make it more or less accessible to students and justify the selection of teaching practices based on learning needs" (p. 257). DI encompasses equity of access to learning opportunities and opens the door to enhanced academic achievement for every student included those from lower socioeconomic communities.

Tomlinson (2014) says, " The teacher in the differentiated classroom believes in the capacity of every student to succeed, works from curriculum that requires every student to grapple with the essential understandings or principles of disciplines and to be a thinker and problem-solver in the context of that curriculum, scaffolds the next steps of every learner in a progression toward and beyond critical learning goals and creates a classroom that actively supports the growth of each of its members" (p. 27). The implications of these considerations in a learning environment speak to equity rather than equality. Students' diverse learning needs demand that they benefit from different instructional strategies. Consequently, excellent opportunities should be created for all students while maintaining the rigor of the curriculum, high expectation for all learners even those from poor communities, using rich resources, diverse teaching strategies and a plethora of assessment strategies to measure learning outcomes or achievement. In this case, not only are students provided with multiple and varied ways to learn, but differentiated approaches to demonstrate their knowledge and its application.

The challenge then, is to effectively deliver impactful instruction to a heterogeneous group of learners in one classroom. Differentiated Instructional approaches should not be viewed as the panacea for effective teaching, but as a possibility. It must be noted that each teacher may have a different philosophy of what constitute differentiation and the amount of the content, product or process to be differentiated or whether all components must be differentiated at the same time to be effective. However, in some schools, teachers have been working in collaboration with their colleagues and with coaches in planning differentiated instructional strategies, incorporating cultural awareness, sharing demographic and assessment data through the media of professional development opportunities and professional learning communities (PLCs) as reported by the principals and teachers in this sample. The respondents when asked how they would explain the high level of success of their schools identified instructional practices. They further highlighted that the use of good assessment data to identify learning needs and inform instructional strategies such as Culturally Relevant and Responsive Pedagogy (CRRP), differentiation, use of technology and use of rich questions as key components of the instruction that supported economically disadvantaged learners. The quantitative data collected indicated high significant correlations with the variables under study. Instructional practices are correlated with leadership (variance 0.914), professional development (variance 0.907) and professional learning communities (0.910). An overall correlation with leadership and all the other variables is variance 0.972. This implies that the more of the variables on which each school demonstrates high significant correlations, the higher the achievement that school will experience. There is no one strategy that will improve achievement for all students, but constant exploration provides hope and possibilities to enhance academic achievement for all.

Culturally Relevant and Responsive Pedagogy (CRRP)

As an instructional strategy, culturally relevant and responsive pedagogy has undergone and continues to undergo transformation and evolution through research and application. Researchers try to understand the concept, the principles, fine tune the strategy and focus the application on enhancing academic achievement for especially learners from disadvantaged backgrounds. Ladson-Billings (1992) purports that culturally relevant pedagogy urges collective action grounded in cultural understanding, experiences and ways of knowing the world. It would seem that educators and researchers focussed on a narrow definition of "culture" which would influence the understanding and the application of the strategy consequently, impacting students' learning outcomes. Therefore, the literature consists of many descriptions of the pedagogy including: culturally relevant, culturally sensitive, culturally centred, culturally congruent, culturally reflective, culturally mediated and now culturally relevant and responsive. (Ladson-Billings, 1992; Au, 1993)

Gay (2000) concludes that culture determines the way individuals think, believe and behave. Therefore, culture is a student's beliefs, motivations, social identity and norms of operation. Teachers' knowledge of the cultural underpinnings influencing thinking, belief and behaviour should impact the decisions to differentiate the instructional strategies. Recognizing the limitations placed on the definitions, descriptions, understanding and applications of the various iterations of culturally relevant pedagogy and the dynamism of cultures, McCauley (2018) offers an expansion of the definition to include: social, physical, mental, gender, sexual orientation, financial status and previous knowledge (p.3). This expanded definition has shed new light on this instructional strategy and has prompted additional research since teachers' mandate is to achieve enhanced academic achievement for all the diverse learners in their classrooms. The characteristics outlined in culturally relevant and responsive pedagogy are: validating and affirming---acknowledging the strengths in the diversity of each student's culture; comprehensive---using cultural resources to teach knowledge, skills, values and attitudes; multidimensional---applies diverse learning theories and approaches to the classroom environment, teaching strategies, assessment and evaluation; empowering--- developing academic competence, personal confidence and courage and lastly, transformative--- defying stereotypes, low expectations, negative thinking and to strive for excellence and to demonstrate resilience (Gay, 2019; 2013; Lipman,1995).

These characteristics should permeate and be evident in all classrooms if student achievement must be maximized. There will continue to be differences in the understanding and applications of the strategy, but an effort should be made to consistently develop teacher exposure and expertise in implementing CRRP. Principal respondents in this study identified CRRP as one of the instructional strategies responsible for the high level of success experienced by their schools serving students from poor communities. Their responses include, "Most teachers use CRRP, use good assessment data to inform instruction, have growth mindsets and hold high expectations for all students, connect students' histories and experiences to the curriculum and plan instructions using Social Justice Lens". Fifty-seven percent (57%) of the teachers surveyed believed that instructional practices contributed to student academic achievement. They believed that the teaching and learning environment should be inclusive, should promote the intellectual engagement of all students and should reflect the individual strengths, needs, learning preferences and cultural perspectives of each students.

The characteristics coupled with the principles of culturally relevant and responsive pedagogy point to a paradigm shift that is transformative in teaching and learning. The principles include: identity development, equity and excellence, developmental appropriateness and teaching the whole child. Identity development includes both teachers and students' educational, cultural and socioeconomic realities and how these realities shape their self-esteem and influence their behaviour. For the teachers, the impact these realities have on their instructional practices and how students' realities inform the learning opportunities provided are points to contemplate. For students from economically disadvantaged backgrounds, the way these realities influence their self-worth, mindset about learning, motivation and interests are factors for careful considerations in designing instructional strategies to meet their learning needs. If learning must be maximized, teachers as well as students should reflect on their identities, acknowledge, value and excellence and capitalize on the influence they have on each other. The students may need some assistance through the social justice approach to extrapolate this knowledge, but the understanding gleaned can be beneficial to the students, their peers and teachers as they cooperatively work on a trajectory to change underachievement to high achievement.

It should be noted that equity and excellence are mutually inclusive principles that should characterize all learning opportunities and should reflect content consisting of positive inclusion of students' family compositions, cultures, socioeconomic realities and ethnicities among other variables. The schools sampled in this study reflected a very diverse population with between 50% and 80% of the students from African heritage as the largest group. Respondents to the interview question when asked to address their student population, demography and the strengths these diverse learners bring to the learning environment reported that there were 33 different languages represented in the schools, many students designated as special needs learners, but exhibited high level of motivation, high sense of responsibility, possessed strong oral language skills and seemed to enjoy learning. The students, at an early age seemed to view schools as positive paces. These schools were diverse and similar in the population they served to some others that were underachieving.

Consequently, implementing curriculum and instructional strategies inclusive of students' backgrounds and lived experience acknowledges that students are different, have different learning needs and require a variety of strategies to maximize their full potentials. The strengths each student brings to the learning environment should then shape the rigor of the curricular experiences and portray high expectations for each student while implementing a Ministry of Education mandated curriculum with its expectations.

Another principle of CRRP is developmental appropriateness. This includes learning styles, teaching strategies and cultural variation of psychological needs--- motivation, morale, engagement and collaboration (Brown-Jeffy and Cooper, 2011). Since there is the recognition that no group of students is monolithic, effective teaching should incorporate strategies to capture a variety of learning styles: multiple intelligences, cooperative learning with mixed abilities, ethnicities, socioeconomic backgrounds and provides opportunities for sharing and developing new knowledge. Here teachers can use direct instructions to set the contextual framework to disseminate pertinent and relevant information to facilitate equal access to information and use rich questions to guide the learning process. The teacher can also use the guided instructional approach to stimulate thinking, encourage discussion, discovery and the creation of new knowledge. This approach also helps in the developing of students' independence, cooperation and creativity. Through the teaching and learning strategies employed there is potential to draw on the wealth of the strengths in students' diversity to enhance academic achievement. Every strategy does not have to be included in every lesson to be effective. However, there should be many and varied strategies to be effective.

The final CRRP principle for consideration is teaching the whole child. This principle addresses the idea that students' out- of- school realities such as SES impact on learning.

Brown-Jeffy and Cooper (2011) conclude that in teaching the whole child, educators must be cognizant of the socio- cultural influences on their learning and account for these influences in designing curriculum and determining pedagogy. CRRP focuses on the academic and personal successes of students as individuals and as a collective and aims at ensuring that students are engaged in academically rigorous curriculum and learning. Students should then possess enhanced understanding, feel affirmed in their identities, experiences and empowered to identify and dismantle structural inequities and transform society (Escudero, 2019). CRRP also embraces a comprehensive knowledge of each student assessment, demographic and community characteristics, intelligences, learning styles among others. This knowledge is pertinent in the designing and delivery of instruction. This instructional strategy provides opportunities for teachers to explore cultural similarities and strengths, examine the power and privileges associated with these different lived experiences, develop knowledge, inquiry and critical thinking through the use of rich questions in an inclusive environment. In this atmosphere students can value their experiences, develop pride in their identity, view themselves with growth mindsets as individuals who can learn, contribute significantly to knowledge development and later societal advancement. In this inclusive climate all students can experience enhanced self-esteem which is critical and important for especially those students trying to challenge stereotypes, develop resilience, cope with traumatic experiences and keep their focus on academic achievement.

Schools can change the path to success for students from economically disadvantaged backgrounds through the use of rich curriculum that highlights differences in cultures, socioeconomic status, languages and learning styles. The opportunities can be created for teachers and students to investigate and create new realities. Students can problem solve independently and in cooperative learning groups where different strengths are present, different roles and responsibilities are assigned on a rotating basis. Students can also be given differentiated opportunities to demonstrate their learning through the arts, presentations, report writing, poetry and other forms congruent with students' preferences. Teachers can through lesson consolidation, provide knowledge expansion, immediate feedback and additional opportunities to students who have not yet mastered the learning objectives. Peer constructive evaluation can also be encouraged in this environment. Both teachers and students stand a chance to benefit significantly. Academic achievement for students from poor communities can therefore be positively impacted.

While there can be no claim that CRRP as an instructional strategy is the only remedy for underachievement challenges, the characteristics and principles if fully understood, carefully incorporated and applied should make a difference in teachers' attempts to accomplish enhanced academic achievement. The schools in the sample have all reported the use of this strategy and have all portrayed significant student achievement on EQAO tests in reading, writing and mathematics.

Use of Technology

Respondents to the principals' interviews identified "use of technology" as another instructional strategy associated with the high level of academic achievement experienced by their schools. They claimed that model schools funds helped to provide additional resources such as computers, laptops and tablets.[1] Principals reported that teachers had been integrating technology in their instructional strategies to provide extended curricular offerings to their students as many students did not have direct access to those resources at home. At school, students are afforded opportunities to explore and apply subject materials in a variety of contexts, compare and contrast ideas, research, create new knowledge and document their findings after careful analysis, synthesis and evaluation. This approach allows students to access a wealth of pertinent and relevant information at their finger tips. Teachers use technology to differentiate the instruction, personalize the activities, pose rich questions, trigger higher order thinking and provide immediate feedback as part of the formative and summative evaluations.

Richardson and Mancabelli (2016) note the benefits of incorporating technology in teaching and learning as follows: increased student

---

[1] Inner-City Model Schools: Underachieving schools located in challenging communities chiefly affected by violence and poverty. These schools attract human and financial resources to support initiatives aimed at improving student achievement.

engagement, improved teacher pedagogy, personalized-paced learning, increased peer feedback, collaborative learning, differentiated learning and communication. They believe that technology enhances learning experiences and provides opportunities to increase student engagement as teachers use a constructivist approach to help students write and problem solve. Students' learning can be personalized and their work saved on their devices to be retrieved for completion at a different time. Students can do additional research, expand on their previous ideas, clarify and even change their ideas. Students can collaborate with their classmates on projects and assignments. Students can use different equipment and apps to demonstrate their learning (Rogers, 2011b).

The use of technology can support student engagement, differentiated instruction, personalized student learning, student collaboration, communication, assessment and feedback. These aspects of the teaching and learning strategies should help to enhance academic achievement for all students including those adversely affected by poverty.

The Use of Rich Questions

Questioning technique is an instructional strategy utilized by many teachers for different purposes. Questioning is used to get students' attention, diagnose understanding, structure and redirect learning and keep students engaged (Stronge and Xu, 2016). Questions can help teachers determine the level of student understanding prior to, during and after the instruction. Information gleaned at these instructional phases become pertinent to diagnosing learning readiness, influence instructional strategies and shape any additional learning opportunities that maybe provided. Consequently, questions should require more than simple recalling facts although there is a place for these questions in learning. Rich questions should allow students to make connections-- imagine, describe, compare, contrast, predict, invent, explain, summarize and problem solve. According to Huinker and Freckman (2004) rich questions allow students to connect, elaborate, evaluate and justify, communicate their thinking, deepen their understanding and extend their learning. Rich questions should be logically linked to curricular expectations, learning goals and success criteria.[2] They should require some lower and higher order thinking skills to provide an entry point to the learning tasks for all students. This strategy could serve as motivation and encouragement as students delve into unpacking complex issues and solve challenging problems. Rich questions should be culturally relevant in order to connect students' experiences consequently, allowing them a reference point to make inferences. Rich questions should be open. Open questions encourage a multiplicity of responses and approaches to problem solving and afford students the opportunities to explore ideas, share perspectives, learn with and from their teachers and peers. Vogler (2008) considers rich questioning as a valuable tool to motivate, engage, evaluate student learning, develop their thinking, stimulate inquiry and investigation. The principal respondents believed the use of rich questions impacted the academic achievement of students living in poverty attending their schools. They said teachers provided rich tasks with multiple entry points to the activities and lessons were focused on higher order thinking skills, but allowed for students to be successful at different levels and to expand their learning.

It can be deduced from the responses that all the schools were using rich questions, culturally relevant and responsive pedagogy, differentiated instruction and technology as part of their repertoire of strategies to enhance achievement. There seems to be an interrelationship among the strategies employed and in some respects a link established to the constructivist learning theories. Small (2008)

---

[2] **Learning goals** are brief statements that describe for students what they should know, understand and be able to do by the end of a period of instruction such as a lesson. They represent a subset or cluster of knowledge and skills that students must master in order to successfully achieve the overall expectations.

Success criteria describe in specific terms and in language meaningful to students, what successful attainment of the learning goals looks like once they have learned. Quality success criteria make learning explicit and transparent for students and teachers alike. They identify the significant aspects of student performance that are assessed and or evaluated (i.e. the "look-fors") in relation to curriculum expectations.

says, "In a constructivist classroom, students are recognized as the ones who are actively creating their own knowledge" (p.3) Teachers using rich questions can help students identify their thinking process, make connections with ideas and create new knowledge and understanding. Teachers can then assess what students have learned and plan the next instructional steps. Instructional practices draw their strengths from many learning theories. These learning theories can be categorized as: behaviourist that is based on the idea that knowledge is dependent on stimuli exterior of the learner. The learner's responds to stimuli is generally passive and the learning is chiefly through repetition and memorization. Cognitivist theories focus on the idea that learners process information and use the information to produce learning outcomes. The Humanist or Motivational theories focus on the whole person and espouse the idea that learners bring values and personal perspectives to the learning environment and that the learning environment should be learner centred and personalized to meet the needs of the individual learner. The Instructivist theories portray the idea that knowledge is transferred from the teacher to the learner and imply that the learner is an empty vessel that comes to the learning environment to be filled. These theorists view learners as passive, emphasize drills, practices and memorization. Lastly, Constructivist theories premise their ideas on the learner centred approach, view students as capable, that is, not with a deficit mindset, but with a growth mindset, value students' cultures, connect each student with his or her previous knowledge, stimulate each learner's participation and create motivational opportunities to encourage learning (Leader in Me, 2018).

All learning theories have their merits and influence the way teachers teach and students learn. However, since all the respondents in this sample reported using culturally relevant and responsive pedagogy, differentiated instruction and rich questions as effective instructional strategies and there seems to be an overlap of the principles underpinning the strategies and their applications, I recommend a careful exploration and consideration of the constructivist theories. Our classrooms are very diverse. Students come from different backgrounds represent different socioeconomic, social, emotional and intellectual experiences. They have different learning needs and styles. These students are capable, their differences should be valued, learning opportunities should place them at the centre and enlist their participation as individuals and cooperatively. Therefore, instructions incorporating constructivist theories should greatly benefit students from lower SES.

There are many factors that impact on teachers' instructional practices. In Ontario, there is the provincial prescribed curriculum with grade level expectations and outcomes accompanied by intended accountability mechanisms such as EQAO tests at grades three, six and nine. There are also graduation requirements at the completion of grade twelve. The environment in which the formal curriculum is delivered is also impacted by the informal or hidden curriculum which is informed by teachers' perceptions, attitudes and behaviours. These aspects of the informal curriculum hold strong views of students, their motivation and capabilities—strengths they bring to the learning tasks.

The most relevant group of learners for this project is students from lower SES. They populate many of our current elementary schools. Their learning should be facilitated through guidance in a supported culture where inquiry is valued, uncertainty and ambiguity tolerated and failure at an attempt is viewed as a welcome strategy to gain a higher level of success. In this learning environment, teachers can challenge and stretch students' thinking using open-ended tasks that are complex, authentic, relevant and self -directed with multiple entry points for success and motivation. Pedagogically, this creates opportunities for both teachers and students to co-construct the success criteria, determine the learning processes, agree on authentic descriptive feedback loops and specify opportunities for remediation.

The final factor that impacts on instructional practices to be considered in this research is learning theories that shape the teaching and assessment strategies. Two of the theories are instructionism and constructionism.

The philosophical under-pinning that governs the instructivist theory is the idea that information and knowledge are transferred from teacher to the learners and result in a change of behaviour, attitude and belief. (Olufemi, 2008) The theory implies a direct transfer of knowledge without any higher order or critical thinking and problem-solving by the learners. The instructivist approach views students as passive information absorbers and emphasizes drills, practices and memorization. However, based on the needs and styles of the learners who populate our classrooms, teachers should explore and utilize different approaches to effect changes in learning and academic achievement for all learners. Since the instructivist approach does not lend itself to self-discovery among other valuable learning skills and is not learner centred, careful consideration should be given to the incorporation of the constructivist approach to learning. The intent is to keep aspects of the instructivist approach that work, but develop a repertoire of strategies commensurable with students' needs.

The constructivist approach embraces the reality that each learner is actively engaged in the construction of knowledge and possesses the capability to comprehend, analyse, synthesize and evaluate information. Instructional strategies based on this approach, are learner-centred, advocates learning in meaningful contexts, promotes problem-based activities and facilitates learners' interactions with their peers (Nikitina, 2010). In this context, teachers operate as facilitators and students are afforded the opportunities to meaningfully connect their present learning with their previous knowledge and experiences. The incorporation and valuing of students' experiences in curricular offerings and pedagogy, establish relevance, stimulate students' participation, motivation and learning. Students from poor communities need to see themselves reflected in all classroom activities. These activities should be used to challenge thinking, stereotypes, myths and propel students to construct and solidity growth mindsets consequently, influencing their learning outcomes.

Figure 2.1 compares the instructivist and constructivist classrooms and provides assumptions about knowledge, students and learning.

Figure 6.1 Instuctivist Versus Constructivist Classrooms

Traditional Classroom	Constructivist Classroom
Curriculum begins with the parts of the whole. Emphasizes basic skills.	Curriculum emphasizes big concepts, beginning with the whole and expanding to include the parts.
Strict adherence to fixed curriculum is highly valued.	Pursuit of student questions and interest is valued.
Materials are primarily textbooks and workbooks.	Materials include primary sources of material and manipulative materials.
Learning is based on repetition.	Learning is interactive, building on what the student already knows.
Teachers disseminate information and students are recipients of knowledge.	Teachers have a dialogue with students, helping students construct their own knowledge.
Teacher's role is directive, rooted in authority	Teacher's role is interactive, rooted in negotiation
Assessment is through testing, correct answers	Assessment includes student works, observations, and points of view, as well as tests. Process is as important as product.
Knowledge is seen as inert.	Knowledge is seen as dynamic, ever changing with our experiences.
Students work primarily alone.	Students work primarily in groups.

(Bada, 2015)

The pedagogical goals of the constructivist classroom can be summarized as: providing experience with the construction of knowledge process and an appreciation of multiple perspectives, embed learning in realistic contexts (authentic tasks), encourage ownership and voice in the learning process, embed learning in social experience (collaboration), encourage multiple teaching and learning and assessment strategies and tools that encourage reflection and metacognition

(Honebein, 1996).

The constructivist approach affords students the opportunities to be actively engaged in their learning, take ownership for the outcome, collaborate with other students by sharing ideas and negotiating alternatives, develop new understanding and higher thinking. Collaborative skills are necessary for learning and success at work. These skills are also very important for students to compete in a global economy. Therefore, a collaboration of both instructivist and constructivist approaches should serve our learners well and assist teachers in their attempts to meet students' diverse learning needs and in their preparation for life.

BIBLIOGRAPHY

Ainsworth, J. " Why Does It Take a Village? The Mediation of Neighbourhood Effects on Educational Achievement". *Social Forces*, 81(1), (2002): 117-152.

Anzovina, T. and Boutilier, D. *Walk A Mile: Experiencing and Understanding Diversity in Canada,* Nelson Education, 2015.

Apple, M. and Beyer, L. *The Curriculum: Problems, Politics and Responsibilities*, Albany: State University of New York Press, 1998.

Au, K. H. *Literacy Instruction in Multicultural Settings,* New York, Harcourt Brace, 1993.

Azzolini, D. and Contini, D. "Performance and Decision: Immigrant-native Gaps in Educational Transition in Italy. *Journal of Applied Statistics,* 48(1),(2016): 98-114.

Bada, S.O." Constructivism Learning Theory: A Paradigm For Teaching and Learning. *IOSR Journal of Research and Methods in Education*, Volume 5, Version 1, (2015): 66-70.

Bambrick-Santoyo, P. *Leaverage Leadership: A Practical Guide to Building Exceptional Schools*, San Francisco, Jossey-Bass, 2012.

Bass, L. and Faircloth, S.C. *Building Bridges from High Poverty Communities, to Schools to Productive Citizenship: A Holistic Approach to Addressing Poverty through Exceptional Leadership*, Peter Lang, Washington, DC., 2013.

Baydar, N. and Brooks-Gunn, J. "Effects of Maternal Employment and Child-care Arrangements on Preschoolers' Cognitive and Behavioural Outcomes: Evidence from the Children of National Longitudinal Survey of Youth". *Developmental Psychology* 27(6), (1991): 932.

Bergeson, T. "Race, Poverty and Academic Achievement", 2006. htt:// www.doh.wa.gov/SBOH/ESS/documents/Race&poverty.pdf

Bhargavi, S. and Yaseem, A. Leadership Styles and Organizational Performance. *Strategic Management Quarterly*, 4(1), 87-117, 2016.

Birky, V.D., Shelton, M. and Headley, S. "An Administrator's Challenge: Encouraging Teachers to be Leaders", *NASSP Bulletin*, 90(2), (2006): 87-101.

Blackstein, A. M. and Noguera, P. *Excellence Through Equity: Five Principles of Courageous Leadership to Guide Achievement for Every Student*, Thousand Oaks, CA, SAGE Publications Ltd.2015.

Blackwell, L. Trezesniewski, K. and Dweck, C. "Implicit Theories of Intelligence Predict Achievement Across an Adolescent Transition: A Longitudinal Study and as Intervention". *Child Development*, 78, (2007): 246-263.

Blasé, J. and Blase, J. "Effective Instructional Leadership: Teachers' Perspectives on How Principals Promote Teaching and Learning in Schools". *Journal of Educational Administration*,(38)2, (2000):130-141.

Bomer, R., Dworin, J., May, L., and Semingson, P. What's Wrong With A Deficit Perspective?" *Teachers' College Records*. (2009). Retrieved from http//www.tcrecord.org (ID No.15648.

Bransford, J., Brown, A., Cocking, R. *How People Learn: Brain, Mind, Experience and School._*Washington DC: National Research Council, 2000.

Brooks-Gunn, J and Duncan, G.J "The Effects of Poverty on Children, *Future of Children*, 7(2), (2007): 55-71.

Brown-Jeff, S. and Cooper, J. E. "Toward a Conceptual Framework of Culturally Relevant Pedagogy: An Overview of the Conceptual and Theoretical Literature". *Teacher Education Quarterly,* V38 N1, (2011): 65-84.

Brown, L. I. "A Meta-Analysis of Research on Influence of Leadership on Student Outcomes", Unpublished Ph. D., Virginia Polytechnic Institute and State University, VA, 2001.

Bryk, A.S., Sebring, P.B., Allensworth, E., Luppescu, S. and Easton, J. Q. *Organizing Schools For Improvement: Lessons From Chicago.* Chicago, University of Chicago Press, 2010.

Burton, P., Phipps, S. and Zhang, L."From Parent to Child: Emerging Inequalities in Incomes for Children in Canada and the U.S". *Child Indicators Research*, 6(2), (2013): 363-400.

Caine, G. And Caine, R.N.*Strengthening and Enriching Your Professional Learning Community: The Art Of Learning Together,* ASCD, Alexandria, VA, 2010.

Campbell, C. "Developing Teachers' Professional Learning: Canadian Evidence and Experiences in a world of Educational Improvement". *Canadian Journal of Education*, 40 (2), (2017): 1-33.

Carey, D. "Improving Educational Outcomes in Germany, France and Paris". OECD Publishing, 2008.

Carter, D. "Achievement as Resistance: The Development of a Critical Race Achievement Ideology among Black Achievers". *Howard Educational Review*, 78(3), (2008): 466-497.

City, E.A., Elmore, R. F., Fiarman, S. E. and Teitel, L. *Instructional Rounds in Education: A Network Approach to Improving Teaching and Learning,* Harvard Education Press, Cambridge, MA, 2011.

Cole, R. *More Strategies for Educating Everybody's Children.* ASCD, Alexandria, VA, 2001.

Cole, R. *Educating Everybody's Children: Diverse Teaching Strategies for Diverse Learners, revised and Expanded 2ⁿᵈ. Edition*, ASCD, Alexandria, VA, 2008.

Collins, D. P., Bruce, J. and McKee, K. Teaching Transformative Leadership for Social Justice: Using Literature Circles to Enhance Learning and Create Deeper Meaning, *Journal of Leadership Education*, Vol. 18, Issue 3, 2019.

Comber, B. "Teachers as Researchers: A Fair Dinkum Learning Legacy". *English in Australia,* 48(3), (2013): 54-61.

Comer, J. P. "Educating Poor Minority Children", *Scientific America*, 259 (5), (1998): 24-30.

Coughlan, S. " How Canada Become an Education Superpower" BBC News.(2017). https//www.bbc.com/news/business-40708421.

Crandall, L and Finn-Miller, S. "Effective Professional Development for Language Teachers". Celce-Marcia, M.; Brinton, D. M. and Snow, M. A. (eds.) *Teaching ESL or Foreign Language,* 4ᵗʰ Edition, (2014):630-648.

Creswell, J.W. *Educational Research: Planning, Conducting and Evaluating Quantitative and Qualitative Research,* Columbus, OH, Pearson-Merrill-Prentice Hall, 2003.

Creswell, J.W. *Qualitative Inquiry and Research Design: Choosing Among Five Approaches,* SAGE Publications Ltd., London, UK, 2013.

Curtis, R. and City, E.A. *Strategies in Action: How School System Can Support Powerful Learning and Teaching,* Cambridge, MA, Harvard Education Press,2009.

Danielson, C. *Teacher Leadership,* ASCD, Alexandria, VA, 2006.

Dougherty, E. and Barth, P. "How to Close the Achievement Gap". *Education Week*, (1997): 40,44.

DuFour, R., Eaker, R. and DuFour, R. "Recurring Themes of Professional Learning Communities and the Assumptions They Challenge". DuFour et.al..(eds) *On Common Grounds: The Power of Professional Learning Communities*. Bloomington, IN, National Education Service, 2005.

DuFour, R., and Eaker, R. *Professional Learning Communities at work: Best Practices for Enhancing Student Achievemen*t, Bloomington, IN, Solution Tree Press,1998.

DuFour, R.; DuFour, R.; Eaker, R. and Karhanek, G. *Raising the Bar and Closing the Gap: Whatever It Takes.* Bloomington, IN., Solution Tree Press, 2010.

DuFour, R. and Fullan, M. *Cultures Built to Last: Systemic PLCs at Work*, Bloomington, IN., Solution Tree Press, 2013.

Duncan-Andrade, J. M. R. *The Art of Critical Pedagogy: Possibilities for moving from Theory to Practice in Urban Schools.* New York, NY, Peter Lang, 2008.

Dweck, C.S. *Mindset: The New Psychology of Success*. New York, NY: Random House, 2006.

Dweck, C. "The Perils and Promises of Praise". *Educational Leadership*, 65(2), (2007): 34-39.

Eaker, R. and Keating, J. *Every School, Every Team, Every Classroom: District Leadership for Growing Professional Learning Communities At Work*, Bloomington, IN: Solution Tree, 2012.

Earl, L. *Assessment As Learning: Using Classroom Assessment to Maximize Student Learning,* Thousand Oaks, CA, Corwin Press, 2003.

Edmonda, R. "Effective Schools for the Urban Poor", *Educational Leadership,*(October), (1979): 15-24

Eizardirad, A. Decolonizing Educational Assessment Ontario Elementary Students and the EQAO. Ph.D. Thesis, University of Toronto, OISE, 2018.

Elmore, R. F. "Building a New Structure for School Leadership". *Cambridge Journal of Education,* 33(3), (2000): 329-351.

Entrof, H. and Minoiu, N. " What a Difference Immigration Policy Makes: A Comparison of PISA Scores in Europe and Traditional Countries of Immigration", *German Economic Review,* 6(3), (2005): 355-373.

Erkens, C., Jakicic, C., Jessie, L.G., King, D., Kramer, S. and Many, T. W. *The Collaborative Teacher: Working Together as a Professional Learning Community.* Bloomington, IN, Solution Tree Press, 2008.

Erkens, C. and Twadell, E. *Leading By Design: An Action Framework for PLC at Work Leaders,* Bloomington, IN. Solution Tree Press, 2012.

Erickson, K., Drevets, W., andSchulkin J. "Glucocorticoid' Regulation of Diverse Cognitive Functions in Normal and Pathological Emotional States". *Neuroscience and Biobehavioural Review,* 27, (2003): 233-246.

Ervay, S. "Academic Leadership in America's Public Schools", NASSP Bulletin, 90(2), (2006):77-86.

Escudero, B. (2019) "How to Practice Culturally Relevant Pedagogy". *Teach For America,* Retrieved en.m.wikipedia.org. 2019.

Evans, G. W. "The Environment of Childhood Poverty, American Psychologist, 59(2), (2004): 77-92.

Evans, G. W. and Kantrowitz, E. "Socioeconomic Status and Health: The Potential Role of Environmental Risk Exposure". *Annual Review of Public Health,* 23, (2002): 303-331.

Evans, G. W.; and Schamberg, M. A. "Childhood Poverty, Chronic Stress, and Adult Working Memory", *Proceedings of the National Academy of Success of the United States of America,* 106, (16), (2009): 6545-6549.

Fenton, B. " New Leaders For Schools: Forming Aligned Instructional Leadership Teams"(12/07/2016), ASCD Express.

Fagan, J. "Income and Cognitive Stimulation as Moderators of the Association between Family Structure and Preschoolers' Emerging Literacy and Math. *Journal of Family Issues,* 38(17), (2017): 2400-2424.

Ferguson, B. T., Tilleczek, K., Boydell, K., Rummens, A. and Reth, E. D. "Early School Leavers: Understanding the lived Reality of School Disengagement From Secondary School—Final Report", 2007.

Ferguson, B., Bovaird, S. and Mueller, M.P. ``The Impact of Poverty on Educational Outcomes for Children", *Paediatrics And Child Health*, 12, (8), (2007): 701-706.

Fullan, M., Hill, P. and Crevola, C. *Breakthrough,* Thousand Oaks, CA, SAGE Publication, 2006.

Fullan, M. "Michael Fullan response to MS 3 questions about personalized learning", 2009. htt://www.micheal fullan.ca/media/13458631.htmi

Fullan, M. *The Six Secrets of Change: What the Best Leaders do to help their Organizations Survive and Thrive,* San Francisco: Jossey-Bass, 2008.

Fullan, M. *The New Meaning of Educational Change*, New York, NY Teachers College Press, 2007.

Fullan, M. *Leading in a Culture of Change,* San Francisco, Jossey Bass, 2001.

Fullan, M. "Choosing the Wrong Drivers for Whole System Reform", 2010a, Centre for Strategic Education Seminar Series Paper 24 @www.case.edu.ca

Fullan, M. *Motion Leadership*, Crown Press, Thousand Oaks, CA, 2010b.

Fullan, M. "Leadership from the Middle: A System Strategy", *Canadian Education Association*, 2015.

Fulton, K. and Britton, T. "STEM Teachers in Professional Learning Communities: From Good Teaching to Great Teaching". *National Commission on Teaching and America's Future*, Washington, DC, 2011.

Gardner, H. *Frames of Mind*, New York: Basic Books, 1983.

Gay, G. "Teaching To and Through Cultural Diversity", Curriculum Inquiry, Volume 43, Issue 1, (2013).

Gay, G. *Culturally Responsive Teaching, 2ⁿᵈ. Ed.*, New York, NY. Teachers College Press, 2010.

Gay, G. *Becoming Multicultural Educators: Personal Journey Toward Professional Agency.* San Francisco, CA: Jossey-Bass, 2003.

Gay, G. *Culturally Responsive Teaching: Theory, Research and Practice,* Teachers College Press, Columbia University, 2000.

Germano, M. A. Leadership Style and Organizational Impact. http://ala-apa.org/newsletter/2010/06/08/spotlight/ 2010.

Gess-Newsome, J. "Pedagogical Content Knowledge". *International Guide to Student Achievement,* New York, Routledge, (2013): 257-259.

Giroux, H. Schooling, Popular Culture and a Pedagogy of Possibility, *SAGE Journal,* 1988.

Glaze, A. and Campbell, C. "Putting Literacy and Numeracy first using research and evidence to support improved student achievement" Ontario Ministry of Education, 2007.

Grant, H. and Dweck, C. "Clarifying Achievement Goals and Their Impact". *Journal of Personality and Social Psychology*, 85, (3), (2003): 541-552.

Good, C.; Rathan, A. and Dweck, C. "It's Ok- Not Everyone Can Be Good at Math: Instructors With an Entity Theory Comfort (and demotivate) Student". *Journal of Experimental Social Psychology*, 48, (2012): 731-737.

Goodwin, B. *Simply Better: Doing What Matters Most to Change the Odds for Student Success, ASCD*, Alexandria, VA, 2011.

Gore, J. M.; Griffiths, T.; and Ladwig, J. G. "Towards Better Teaching: Productive Pedagogy as a Framework for Teacher Education", *Teaching and Teacher Education*, 20(4), (2004): 375-387.

Haberman, M. "The Pedagogy of Poverty Versus Good Teaching". *Phi Delta Kappan, 73 (4), (1991):* 290-294.

Hall, P. and Simeral, A. *Building Teachers' Capacity For Success: A Collaborative Approach for Coaches and School Leaders,* Alexandria, VA, 2008.

Hallinger, P. "Leading Educational Change: Reflections on the Practice of Instruction and Transformational Leadership", *Cambridge Journal of Education*, 33(3), (2003): 329-351.

Hammond, Linda-Darling. "Educational Leadership: A Bridge to School Reform," The Wallace Foundation National Conference, New York City, (2007): October22-24.

Hannay, L. Wideman, R. and Seller, W. "Professional Learning to Reshape Teaching". *Toronto Elementary Teachers Federation of Ontario,* 2010.

Hansushek, E. A. "The Economics of School Quality", *German Economic Review,* 6(3), (2005): 269-286.

Hargreaves, A. and Frank, D. *Sustainable Leadership.* San Francisco, Jossey Boss, 2006.

Hargreaves, A. and Fullan, M. "Reviving Teaching with Professional Capital). *Education, Week,* Vol. 31, Issue 33,(2012): 30-36.

Hargreaves, A., and Braun, H. "Leading for All: A Research Report of the Development, Design, Implementation and Impact of Ontario's "Essential for Some, Good for All" Initiative. Toronto, ON: Council of Ontario Directors of Education, 2011.

Hargreaves, A., Shirley, D., Wagnia, S., Bacon, C. and D'Angelo M. "Leading from the Middle: Spreading Learning, Well-Being, and Identity Across Ontario". Toronto, ON: Council of Ontario Directors of Education, 2018.

Harris, A. and Chapman, C. "Leadership in Schools", Report to the National College of School Leadership, London, UK, 2001.

Harris, A. and Jones, M. "Professional Learning Communities and System Improvement", *Improving Schools,* Vol.13, No. 2, (2010): 172-181.

Harris, A and Muijs, D. "Teacher Leadership Principles and Practice", *National College for School Leadership (Great Britain),* 2015.

Hattie, J. *Visible Learning: A Synthesis of Over 800 Meta-Analyses Relating to Achievement.* New York, NY, Routledge, 2009.

Hattie, J. *Visible Learning For Teachers: Maximizing Impact on Learning,* New York, NY, Routledge, 2012.

Hattie, J. and Jaeger, R. "Assessment and Classroom Learning: A Deductive Approach" in *Assessment in Education,* Volume 5, No. 1, University of North Carolina, NC, 1998.

Haycock, K." Education Trust Report: Good Teaching Matters….A Lot", *Education Trust*, 3(2), (1998):2-15.

Hodges, H. "Overcoming A Pedagogy Of Poverty". *More Strategies for Educating Everybody's Children, ASCD,* Alexandria, VA., 2001.

Hess, M. and Kelly, A. P. "Learning to Lead: What Gets Thought in Principal Preparation Program", *Teachers' College Record*, 109(1), (2007): 244-247.

Honebein, P.C. "Seven Goals for the Design of Constructivist Learning Environments", Wilson, Brent (ed.) *Constructivist Learning Environments: Case Studies in Instructional Design. Educational Technology Publications,* Englewood Cliffs, New Jersey, 1996.

Hopkins, D. *Meeting the Challenge: An Improvement Guide for Schools Facing Challenging Circumstances.* London: Department of Educational Skills, 2001.

Hord, S. M. *Professional Learning Communities: Communities of Continuous Inquiry and Improvement,* Austin, TX: Southwest Educational Laboratory, 1997.

Howard, G.R. *We Can't Teach What We Don't Know: White Teachers, Multiracial Schools,* Teachers College Press, Columbia University, New York, 2006.

Hoy, A. and Hoy, W. *Instructional Leadership: A Learning Centre Guide,* Boston, MA: Allyn and Bacon, 2003.

Hoy, W.K., Tarter, C.J. and Hoy, A.W. " Academic Optimism of Schools: A Force Foe Student Achievement", *American Educational Research Journal,* 43 (3), (2006): 425-446.

Huinker, D. and Freckman, J. "Conversation to Promote Teacher Thinking". *Teaching Children Mathematics.* (10) 7, (2004): 352-357.

Hulchanski, J.D. "Report: The Three Cities Within Toronto, Income Polarization Among Toronto's Neighbourhoods", Cities Centre and Faculty of Social Work, University of Toronto, 2007.

Inger, M. "Teacher Collaboration in Secondary Schools". *Centre Focus*, No. 2.(1993).

Isaacs, J.B. ``Starting School at a Disadvantage: The School Centre for Children Readiness of Poor Children and Families", Brooking Institute, 2012.

Iqbal, N., Anwar, S. and Haider, N. Effect of Leadership Style on Employee Performance, *Arabian Journal of Business and Management Review*, 5(5), 1-6, 2015.

Isaacs, J. and Magnuson, R. ``Income and Education as Predictors of Children's School Readiness``, Washington, DC, The Brookings Institute, 2011.

Jacobson, S. L., Brooks, S., Giles, C., Johnson, L., and Ylimakl, R. "Successful Leadership in Three High Poverty Urban Elementary Schools". *Leadership and Policy in Schools*, 20(1), (2007): 61-78.

Jensen, E. *Teaching With Poverty in Mind: What Being Poor Does to Kids Brains and What Schools Can Do About It*, ASCD, Alexandria, VA, 2009.

Jensen, E. *Poor Students, Rich Teaching: Mindsets for Change*, IN., Solution Tree Press, 2016.

Jensen, E. *Poor Students, Richer Teaching: Mindsets That Raise Student Achievement*, Bloomington, IN., Solution Tree Press, 2017.

Jacobson, S.L. "Leadership for Success in High Poverty Elementary Schools". *Journal of Educational Leadership, Policy and Practice,* 23(1), (2008): 3-17.

Jakicic, C. "Too Much to Teach: How to Identify What Matters Most". *The Collaborative Teacher: Working Together in Professional*

Learning Community, Bloomington, IN., Solution Tree Press, 2008.

Johnson, J. P., Livingston, M. and Schwartz, R.A. " What Makes A Good Elementary School? A Critical Examination", *Journal of Educational Research*, 93(5), (2000): 32-36.

Johnson, D.S. "Naturally Acquired Learned Helplessness: The Relationship Of School Failure to Achievement Behaviour, Attributions, and Self-Concept". *Journal of Educational Psychology* 73(2), (1981): 174-180.

Johnson-Brooks, C.H., Lewis, M.A., Evans, G.W. and Whalen, C.K. "Chronic Stress and Illness in Children: Role of Allostatic Load". *Psychosomatic Medicine* 60(5), (1998): 597-603

Jyoti, J. and Bhau, S. Impact of Transformational Leadership on Job Performance: Mediating Role of Leader-Member Exchange and Rational Identification. *SAGE Open,* 5(4), 1-13, 2015.

Kagan, S. L. "Readiness Past, Present and Future: Shaping the Agenda". *Young Child,* 48, (1992): 48-53.

Kanold, T. D. *The Five Disciplines of PLC Leaders*, Bloomington, IN, Solution Tree, 2011.

Karten, T. J. *Inclusion Strategies That Work,* Thousand Oaks, CA, Corwin Press, 2015.

Katz, S., Earl, L. M. and Jaafar, S.B. *Building and Connecting Learning Communities: The Power of Networks for School Improvement,* Corwin, California, 2009.

Katzenmeyer, M. and Moller, G. *Awakening the Sleeping Giant: Helping Teachers Develop as Leaders,* Thousand Oaks, CA, Corwin Press, 2001.

Kilgour, D. "Whither Racism?" *Canadian Social Studies* 29, no.1, 6-7, 1994.

Killion, J. and Roy, P. *Becoming a Learning School*, NSCD, New Jersey, 2009.

King, S. "The Limited Presence of African-American Teachers", *Review of Educational Research* 63, no. 2, 115-149, 1993.

Kitchen, R., DePree, J., Caledon-Pittichis, S. and Brinkerhoff, J. "High Achieving School Initiative: Final Report", (2004). http://www.unm.edu/~jbrink/HAS/hp_final_report2.pdf.

Lacour, M. and Tissington, L.D. "The Effects of Poverty on Academic Achievement", *Educational Research and Reviews*, Vol. 6 (7) (2011): 522-527.

Ladson-Billings, G. " Reading Between the Lines *Theory into Practice*. 31 and Beyond the Pages: A Culturally Relevant Approach to Literacy Teaching". (4), (1992): 312-320.

Leadbetter, C. "Learning About Personalization", London Innovation Unit, Department of Education and Sills, 2002.

Liberman, A. and Friedrich, L.D. *How Teachers Become Leaders: Learning From Practice and Research*, New York, NY: Teachers' College Press, 2010.

Liberman, A., Saxl, E. and Miles, M. "Teacher Leadership, Ideology and Practice) *Liberman(ed.), Building a Professional Culture in Schools, T*eachers College Press, (1998): 300-877.

Lipman, P. "Bringing Out the Best in Them". *The Contribution of Culturally Relevant Teaching to Education Reform: Theory into Practice,* 34 (3), (1995): 202-208.

Leithbridge, L. and Phipps, S. "Income and the Outcomes of Children", Analytical Studies Branch Research Paper Series 24-F, 2006.

Leithwood, K "How the Leading Student Achievement Project Improves Student Learning: An Evolving Theory of Action" –Literacy and Numeracy (LNS) Paper, 2010.

Leithwood, K.. Louis, K.S., Anderson, S. and Wahlstrom, K. " learning From Leadership: Investigating the Links to Improved Student Learning", 2010. http://www.wallacefoundation.org/page/abou t-the-organization-learning-from-leadership.aspx

Leithwood, K. A., Steinbach, R. and Jantzi, D. "School Leadership and Teachers Motivation to Implement Accountability Policy", *Education Administration Quarterly*, 38 (1), (2002): 94-119.

Leithwood, K. and Seashore-Louis, K. *Linking Leadership and Improvement to Student Learning*, San Francisco, CA, Jossey-Bass, 2011.

Levin, B. " Schools, Poverty and Achievement Gap". *Phi Delta Kappan*, 89(1), (2007): 75-76.

Levin, B. *How to Change 5000 Schools: A Practical and Positive Approach for Leading Change at Every Level.* Cambridge, MA, Harvard Education Press, 2008.

Lingard, B.; Hayes, D.; and Mills, M. "Teachers and Productive Pedagogies: Contextualizing, Conceptualizing, Utilizing". *Journal of Pedagogy, Culture and Society*, Vol. 11, Issue 3. (2003).

Lous, K.S. and Marks, H.M. "Teacher Empowerment and the Capacity for Organizational Learning", *Educational Administrational Quarterly*, 35(5), (1996): 707-750.

Lupien, S. J., King, S. Meaney M. J. and McEwen, B.S. "Can Poverty Get Under Your Skin? Basal Cortisol Levels and Cognitive Unction in Children From Low and High Socioeconomic Status". *Developmental Psychopathology*, 13 (3), (2001): 653-676.

Ma, X. and Klinger, D. A. "Hierarchical Linear Modeling of Standard School Effects on Academic Achievement", *Canadian Journal of Education*, 25(2), (2000): 41.

Marks, H.M. and Printy, S. M. "Principal Leadership and School Performance: An Investigation of Transformational and Instructional Leadership." *Educational Administrative Quarterly* 39 (3), (2003): 370-397.

Marzano, R., Walters, T. and McNulty, B. *School Leadership That Works: From Research to Results,* Alexandria, VA: ASCD, 2005.

Maslow, A. H. "A Theory of Human Motivation". *Psychology Review*, 50(4), (1943): 370.

McCann, T.M, Jones, A. C. and Aronoff, G. A. *Teaching Matters Most: A School's Guide to Improving Classroom Instruction.* California, Corwin, 2012.

McLeod, J. "An Introduction to Counseling". *Journal of Time Series Analysis* Vol.2, No. 4. (1998).

McCauley, S. "Culturally Relevant and Responsive Pedagogy in The Early Years: It's Never Too Early!" *ETFO Voice*, Elementary Teachers' Federation of Ontario. 2018.

McGregor, D. New York 21, (1960):166-171.

Ministry of Education "Achieving Excellence: A Renewed Vision of Education in Ontario", Queen's Printer of Ontario, Toronto, 2014.

Mistry, R. S., Vanderwater, E. A., Huston, A. C. and Mclloyd, V.C. "Economic Well-being and Children's Social Adjustment: The Role of Family Processes in an Ethnically Diverse Low income Sample". *Child Development*73, (2002): 935-951.

Mitonga-Monga, J. and Coetzee, M. Perceived Leadership Style and Employee Participation, *African Journal of Business Management,* 6(15), 2012.

Muhammad, A. *Transforming School Culture: How to Overcome Staff Division.* Bloomington, IN, Solution Tree Press, 2009.

Muijs, D. and Harris, A. "Teacher Leadership-- Improvement Through Empowerment? An Overview of the Literature". *Educational Management and Administration*, 31, (2003): 437-448.

Murphy, J. "Re-culturing the Profession of Educational Leadership: New Blueprint". *Yearbook of the National Society for the Study of Education*, 101(1), (2002): 65-82.

Murray, J. *The Educational Challenge: Redefining Leadership for the 21ˢᵗ century. Yearbook of the National Society of the Study of Education.* Chicago: University of Chicago Press, (2002): 62-68.

Naylor, N.. "Education That Works For You", Ontario Ministry Of Education Mandate, 2019.

Nikitina, H. "Addressing Pedagogical Dilemmas in a Constructive Language". *Journal of the Scholarship of Teaching and Learning*, Vol. 10, No. 2, (2010): 90-106.

Noble, K. G., Norman, M. F. and Farah, M. J. "Neurocognitive Correlates of Socioeconomic Status in Kindergarten Children", *Developmental Science*, 8(1), (2005): 74-87.

Noguera, P.A. "A Broader and Bolder Approach uses Education to Break the Cycle of Poverty". *Phi Delta Kappan, (2011):* 8-14.

O' Brien, M., McCluskey, K., Dole, S, MacKinlay, E. and Montes, C. " Pre-service Learning and the (gentle) Disruption of Emerging Teaching Identity". J. Faulkner et.al. (ed.), *Disrupting Pedagogies and Teaching the Knowledge Society: Countering Conservative Norms With Creative Approaches.* Sydney: IGI Global, 2012.

OCED. "Building a High-quality Teaching Profession: Lessons from Around the World, Organization for Economic Cooperation and Development", Paris, 2011.

OECD. "Programme for International Student Assessment (PISA)", 2010.

Ojokuku, R. M., Odetayo, T. A. and Ssjuyigbe, A. S. Impact of Leadership Style on Organizational Performance: A Case Study of Nigerian Banks. *American Journal of Business of Management*, 1(4), 202-207, 2012.

Olufemi, O. "Pedagogical Approaches and Technical Subject Teaching Through Internet Media". *The Electronic Journal of e-Learning*, Vol. 6, No.1, 2008: 53-56.

Ontario Ministry of Education. "Me Read? No Way! *A Practical Guide to Improving Boys' Literacy Skills*", Toronto, Ontario: Queen's Printer for Ontario, 2004.

Ontario Ministry of Education. "Many Roots, Many Voices: Supporting English Language Learners in Every Classroom, A Practical Guide for Ontario Educators", 2005.

Ontario Ministry of Education. "Education for All: The Report of the Expert Panel on Literacy and Numeracy Instruction for Students with Special Education Needs, Kindergarten to Grade 6". Toronto, Ontario: Queen's Printer for Ontario, 2005.

Ontario Ministry of Education. "Ontario First Nations, Metis and Inuit Education Policy Framework. Toronto", Ontario: Queen's Printer for Ontario, 2007.

Ontario Ministry of Education. "Building Bridges to Success for First Nations, Metis, and Inuit Students: Developing Policies for Self-Identification: Successful Practices From Ontario School Boards. Toronto", Ontario: Queen's Printer for Ontario, 2007.

Ontario Ministry of Education. "Supporting English Language Learners: A Practical Guide for Ontario Educators Grades 1-8. Toronto", Ontario: Queen's Printer for Ontario. 2008.

Panopto "Are You Ready to Support 4 Generations of Learners"? 2017. https://www.panopto.com.

Paperny, A. M. "The Shrinking Middle Class Makes Toronto a City of Economic Extremes", *The Globe and Mail,* (2010): December 15.

Parret, W. H. and Budge, K.\M. *Turning High-Poverty Schools into High-Performing Schools,* ASCD, Alexandria, Virginia, 2012.

Payne, R. K and Slocumb, P.D. *Boys in Poverty: a Framework for Understanding Dropout,* Bloomington, IN., Solution Tree Press, 2011.

Putnam, R. T. and Borko, H. " What Do New Views of Knowledge and Thinking. Have to Say About Research on Teacher Learning"? *Educational Research*, 29 (1), (2000): 4-5

Quinn, T. "Redefining Leadership in the Standard Era". *Principal*, 82(1), (2002):16-20.

Reason, C and Reason, L. "Asking The Right Questions", *Educational Leadership* 65 (1), (2007): 36-40.

Reeves, D.B. *The Learning Leader: How to Focus School Improvement for Better Results.* ASCD, Alexandria, VA, 2006.

Reeves, D. *From Leading to Succeeding: The Seven Elements of Effective Leadership in Education,* Bloomington, IN., Solution Tree Press, 2016.

Richardson, W. and Mancabelli, R. *Personal Learning Networks: Using the Power of Connection to Transform Education,* Bloomington, IN, Solution Tree Press, 2011.

Reynolds, D., Hopkins, D., Potter, D. and Chapman, C. *School Improvement for Schools Facing Challenging Circumstances: A Review of Research and Practice.* London: Department of Skills, 2001.

Ricci, M.C. *Mindsets in the Classroom: Building a Culture of Success and Student Achievement in Schools,* Prufrock, Press INC, 2013.

Robinson, V. *Student Centred Leadership*, San Francisco, CA, Jossey-Bass, 2011.

Rockoff, J. E. "The Impact of Individual Teachers on Student Achievement: Evidence From Panel Data", *American Economic Review*, 94, (2004):242-252.

Rogers, K. D. *Bring Your Own Device: Engaging Students and Transforming Instruction*, Bloomington, IN, Solution Tree Press, 2016.

Rogers, K. D. "Four Mistakes Educators Make When Integration Technology into Instruction", Web log post, 2011b.

Rohrer, D. and Pashler, H. "Recent Research on Human Learning Challenges Conventional Instructional Strategies", *Educational Researcher*, 39, (2010): 406-412.

Rosenholtz, S.J. *Teachers' Workplace: The Social Organization of Schools*. New York, Teachers College Press, 1991.

Ross, D. and Adam, A. "A Review of Research on the Impact of Professional Learning, School of Teaching and Learning, University of Florida" *Teaching and Teacher Education*, 24, (2008): 80-91.

Rowan, B., Cohen, D.K. and Raudenbush, S.W. " Improving the Educational Outcomes of Students in Poverty Through Multidisciplinary Research and Development", 2004, http://www.isr.umich.edu/carss/about/Prospectus.pdf

Rukmani, K., Ramesh, M. and Jayakrishnan, J. Effects of Leadership Styles on Organizational Effectiveness. *European Journal of Social Sciences*, 15(3) 365-369, 2010.

Sange, P. "Leading Learning Organizations", *Training and Development,* Vol.50, No. 12, (1992): 36-40.

Segeren, A. and Kutsyuruba, B. "Twenty Years and Counting: An Examination of the Development of Equity and Inclusive Education Policy in Ontario". *Canadian Journal of Educational Administration and Policy*, 2012.

Sharrat, L. and Fullan, M. *Realization: The Change Imperative For Deepening District Wide Reform,* Thousand Oaks, CA., Crown Press, 2009.

Shields, C.M. Dialogic Leadership for Social Justice: Overcoming Pathologies of Silence, *Educational Administrative Quarterly*, 40(1), 109-132. 2010.

Shelton, M and Headley, S. "The Role of Teacher Leaders in School Improvement Through the Perceptions of Principals and Teachers". *International Journal of Education,* Vol. 4 (2006).

Small, M. *Making Mathematics Meaningful to Canadian Students K-8, Toronto, Ontario*, Nelson Education, 2008.

Smith, J. R., Brooks-Gunn, J. and Klebanov, P. K. "Consequences of Living in Poverty for young Children's Cognitive and Verbal Ability and Early School Achievement in Duncan, Brook-Gunn (eds.), *Consequences of Growing Up Poor*, New York, Russell Sage Foundation, (1997): 132-189.

Statistics Canada, 2011.

Stein, A " Creating the Context for Growth Mindsets in the Classrooms", *Education Week*, 2014.

Stein, A. "Effects of Prenatal Mental Disorders on the Fetus and Child", *The Lancet* Vol. 384, No. 9956, (2014): 1800-1819.

Stein, M. K. and D'Amico. "The Influence of Principal Leadership on Classroom Instruction and Student Learning: Towards a Theory of Leadership Practice." *Journal of Curriculum Studies*, 36, (2000): 3-34.

Stronge, J. H. and Xu, X. *Instructional Methods for Differentiation and Deeper Learning*, Bloomington, IN, Solution Tree Press, 2016.

TDSB, "Urban Diversity Strategies: Focus on Student Achievement: Raising the Bar and Closing the Gap", 2008.

Teitel, L. "Improving Teaching and Learning through Instructional Rounds", Harvard Educational Letter, Harvard Graduate School of Education, Volume 25, 2009.

Todd, R. *Evidence-based Practice and School Libraries Knowledge Quest,* 43(3), (2015): 8-15.

Truth and Reconciliation Commission " Honouring the Truth, Reconciling for the Future: Summary of the Final Report of the Truth and Reconciliation Commission of Canada. Ottawa, Ontario: TRC, 2015.

Stipek, D. J. "Motivation and Success" in D. C. Berlinder and R. C. Calfee (eds.) *Handbook of Educational Psychology.* New York, McMillan, (1996): 85-113.

Stroll, L., Bolam, R., McMahon, A., Wallace, M. and Thomas, S. " Professional Learning Communities: A Review of Literature" *Journal of Educational Change,* 7, (2006): 221-258.

Teddie, C., and Tashakkori, A. *Foundations of Mixed Methods Research: Integrating Qualitative and Quantitative Approaches in the Social and Behavioral Sciences*, SAGE Publication, Inc, California, 2009.

Stronge, J. H., Richard, H.B. AND Catano, N. *Qualities of Effective Principals,* ASCD, Alexandria, VA, 2008.

Tashakkori, A. and Teddlie, C. "Handbook of Mixed Methods in Social and Behavioural Research", Thousand Oaks. Sage, *Journal of Mixed Methods Research* 1(1), (2003): 3-7

Thomas, E. M. "Readiness to Learn at School Among Five-Year-Old Children in Canada." Report, 2007.

Timerlay, H., Kaser, L. and Halbert, J. "A Framework For Transforming Learning in Schools: Innovation and the Spiral of Inquiry". Melbourne Centre for Strategic Education, Seminar Series Paper No. 234, 2014.

Tomlinson, C. A. *The Differentiated Classroom; Responding To The Needs of All Learners,* ACED, Alexandria, VA, 2014.

Toronto Star. "Child Poverty Rates in Canada, Ontario Remains High", 2013.

----------"Toronto Holds on to its Shameful Title: Child Poverty Capital of Canada", 2015.

Tschanner-Morgan, M. (2004) "Teacher Efficacy: Capturing An Elusive Construct", *Teaching and Teacher Education,* 17(7), (2004): 783-805.

Van de Grift, W. and Houtveen, A. "School Effectiveness and School Improvement", *International Journal of Research*, Vol. 10, Issue 4, 1999.

Vesio, V., Ross, D. and Adams, A. " A Review of Research on the Impact of Professional Learning Communities on Teaching Practice and Student Learning", *An International Journal of Research and Studies*, Vol. 24. No.1, (2008): 80-91.

Vlimaki, R. M. "Toward a New Conceptualization of Vision in the Work of Educational Leadership: A Case of Visionary Archetype", *Educational Administrative Quarterly,* 42 (4), (2006): 620-651.

Vogler, K.E. "Asking Good Questions", *Educational Leadership*, 65(9), 2008.

Volante, L., Schnepf, S. V., Jerrim, J. and Klinger, D. A. *Socioeconomic Inequalities and Student Outcomes: Cross-National Trends, Policies and Practices,* Springer Nature, Singapore Pte. Ltd. 2019.

Vygotsky, L.S. *Mind in Society,* Cambridge, MA: Harvard University Press, 1978.

Willms, J. D. "Ten Hypotheses about Socioeconomic Gradients and Community Differences in Children's Developmental Outcomes". Report SP -560 -01 -03E Applied Research Branch, Human Resources Development, Canada, 2007.

Wilson, D. and Conyers, M. *Teaching Students to Drive Their Brains: Metacognitive Strategies,* Alexandria, VA, ASCD, 2016.

Wink, J. R. *A Leader's Guide to Excellence in Every Classroom: Creating Support System for Teacher Success,* Bloomington, IN., Solution Tree Press, 2017.

Yamauchi, L. A. "Making School Relevant for At-risk Students: The Waianae High School Hawaiian Studies Program". *Journal of Education for Students Placed at Risk,* 8(4), (2003): 375-390.

Ylimaki, R.M. "Instructional Leadership in Challenging US Schools". *International Studies in Educational Administration, CCEAM, 2007.*

York-Barr, J. and Duke, K. "What Do We Know About Teacher Leadership? Findings From Two Decades of Scholarship". *Review of Educational Research,* 74, (2004): 255-3.

Zapeda, S.J. *Professional Development: What Works?* Larchmont, NY: Eye on Education, 2008.